Christian Mission and Social Justice

Samuel Escobar and John Driver

Introduction by R. Pierce Beaver

Institute of Mennonite Studies
Missionary Studies No. 5

HERALD PRESS
Scottdale, Pennsylvania
Kitchener, Ontario

Library of Congress Cataloging in Publication Data

Escobar, Samuel E.
    Christian mission and social justice.

(Missionary studies; no. 5)
    Includes bibliographical references.
    1. Mission of the church—Addresses, essays,
lectures. 2. Christianity and justice—Addresses,
essays, lectures. I. Driver, John, 1924-   joint
author. II. Title. III. Series.
BV601.8.E83   1978   266'.001   78-6035

ISBN 0-8361-1855-3

CHRISTIAN MISSION AND SOCIAL JUSTICE
Copyright ©1978 by Herald Press, Scottdale, Pa. 15683
    Published simultaneously in Canada by Herald Press,
    Kitchener, Ont. N2G 4M5
Library of Congress Catalog Card Number: 78-6035
International Standard Book Number: 0-8361-1855-3
Printed in the United States of America
Design: Alice B. Shetler

10   9   8   7   6   5   4   3   2

Contents

Missionary Study Series

Published by Herald Press Scottdale, Pennsylvania, in association with Institute of Mennonite Studies, Elkhart, Indiana called for correction. Persons in the ecumenical camp have called for making personal salvation central to the task. On the other hand, the children of the North American evangelicals—especially in Latin America— have taught their parents that humanization and development are a part of the salvific work of the gospel and of that total liberation which is the abundant life which our Lord Jesus Christ came to bring to men. It is beginning to be obvious that each of the pair of terms so violently opposed are really supplementary and complementary in a synthesis. This book treats Christian mission *and* social justice, not Christian mission *or* social justice.

Two major aids to the resolution of the conflict and to a truer understanding of the meaning of mission are (1) the reading of the New Testament creatively in light of the world situation in which it was first spoken and the situation in which it is heard today, and (2) a knowledge of the history of missions. The Mennonites are in a key position to reconcile the conflicting forces and to blaze a trail into the new age of world mission. Mennonites are the foremost nonpartisans in the whole missionary enterprise. They are mediators and bridge-builders between the "church missions" and the nondenominational faith missions. Evangelicals know them to be evangelical, and ecumenical churchmen know them to be cooperative churchmen. None would call Mennonites "liberals" or "modernists." No other denomination or confession puts as large a percentage of its personnel and resources into social service and action. Moreover, Mennonites have in their community relationships over the centuries demonstrated the meaning of the forgiveness of sins and the bearing of one another's burdens in Christian love. They have considerable credibility. A new ferment has been introduced recently into missiological thinking by Mennonite biblical perspectives and by bringing a historical critique derived from a reappraisal of the distinctive Mennonite experience in the Reformation. This book makes a notable contribution to both.

The idea that the proper end and goal of mission is solely the offering of personal salvation in the hereafter is a very late view. Individual salvation was always primary in Protestant missionary thought, but never that alone. Mission was always directed to the planting of churches, on the one hand, and to changing the circumstances of the convert, on the other. Social action in mission can be traced from the time of the apostles, but we will deal only with the Protestant world mission. First of all there was always concern to feed the hungry, heal the sick, cleanse the lepers, and bind the wounds of the miserable. Relief was a constant function of missionaries, especially when famine and floods brought suffering, food and clothing were distributed, and starving persons were employed in building roads and levies.

However, concern was never limited to relief. The itinerating missionary carried with him a bag of medicines, new or better seeds and plants, and improved livestock. Nevius introduced the modern orchard industry into Shantung. The Basel missionaries revolutionized the economy of Ghana by introducing coffee and cocoa grown by families and individuals on their own lands. James McKean transformed the life of northern Thailand by eliminating its three major curses—smallpox, malaria, and leprosy. Wells and pure water often came through the help of missionaries. Industrial schools were stressed through the nineteenth century, and industries were established. Salvation was

7

in the here and now, not only in the future life. They were thoroughgoing evangelists who did these things.

Cotton Mather told the American Indians that the motives behind the mission to them were *gloria Dei* and compassion for their perishing souls and for their wretched physical state. Transformation of the social and economic conditions of the Indians was inseparable from preaching and nurture. Unfortunately the missionaries confused the gospel with English/American culture, and tried to make the Indian over into a white man. Rufus Anderson challenged the dual objectives of evangelization and civilization, affirming that the gospel itself would effect social change. But the missionaries generally believed that tremendous social changes were being wrought and that God was bringing in His kingdom through Christian institutions and ministries. James S. Dennis assembled the evidence in the three huge volumes of his *Missions and Social Progress*. The taproot of the Social Gospel Movement is in the overseas missionary enterprise.

There are those who say that the social action of the missionaries was only remedial, and that a concern for justice was not part of it. That is far from the truth. Although they were the beneficiaries of colonialism in a number of particulars, the missionaries were constantly the protectors of native peoples against exploitation and injustice by government and commercial companies. The governor-generals of South Africa referred to them euphemistically as "the blessed missionaries" because of their constant intervention. They played a very important part in the abolishing of forced labor in the Congo. They resisted blackbirding in the South Pacific. They fought fiercely for human rights in combating

8

opium, foot-binding, and exposure of girl babies in China. They waged war against widow-burning, infanticide, and temple prostitution in India, and above all broke the social and economic slavery of the caste system for the low and outcaste peoples. Examples could be multiplied.

The poor and the oppressed have been special objects of mission. The Moravians under Zinzendorf rediscovered mission work as the central task of the church of Christ, and they began with ministry to the black slaves of the Virgin Islands and Surinam. It was the Anglican Evangelicals who established the Church Missionary Society who brought about the abolition of the slave trade. It is popular in some circles today to say that Livingstone was primarily opening Africa for European trade, but his passion was the abolition of the slave trade and he saw the introduction of commerce as the best means of destroying that trade.

The devotion of the missionaries to the poor and oppressed was derived from Jesus Christ Himself. Jesus in the Great Commission as given in Acts promised the gift of the Holy Spirit for witness, and sent His disciples into Jerusalem and Judea and Samaria and to the end of the earth. This directive is usually thought of in geographical terms. However, there is another way of looking at Samaria. The Jews of Judea despised the Samaritans (those mixed breed descendants of the northern kingdom of Israel, heretics) and they treated them as less than human. Every country, every people, every religion has its Samaritans in this sense. A very special witness and ministry to them is appointed by Christ. During the period since World War II this has been rediscovered. Mennonites have been in the forefront of this witness, and as

9

they have been pioneers in action so also they are pioneers in missiological thought and discussion. The Institute of Mennonite Studies is to be congratulated and thanked for its leadership.

R. Pierce Beaver
Professor Emeritus
The Divinity School
The University of Chicago

1

The Need for Historical Awareness

Samuel Escobar

The Controversial Point of Modern Missiology

We do not need to stress that "missions and social justice" is a complex and controversial subject. The controversy has intensified in recent years both among older and younger churches around the world. Take for instance these words from the well-known African leader Burgess Carr:

> Mission boards and missionary societies are perpetrators of structural violence at the deepest level of our humanity in the so-called younger churches, and they should be abolished in order that new relationships may evolve to internationalize the missionary task of the churches.[1]

These are strong words indeed. If any relationship is found here between missions and social justice it is that

11

missions are the enemies of social justice. Mark the expression, "perpetrators of structural violence at the deepest level of our humanity." We are dealing with an explosive subject.

In this first chapter we will approach the problem historically. Our method will be to become aware of the historical distance that mediates between ourselves and some phases of our subject, trying in that way to grasp a vision that may help a more sober reflection about facts.

Two Stories for Reflection

We can start by reading a brief old missionary story and comparing it with a more recent one. The first is distant in geography and time. We find it in Acts 16 where we have the story of how Paul the apostle carried on his missionary task to the city of Philippi. Here we have one incident during that mission:

Once, when we were on our way to the place of prayer, we met a slave-girl who was possessed by an oracular spirit and brought large profits to her owners by telling fortunes. She followed Paul and the rest of us, shouting, "These men are servants of the Supreme God, and are declaring to you a way of salvation." She did this day after day, until Paul could bear it no longer. Rounding on the spirit he said, "I command you in the name of Jesus Christ to come out of her," and it went out there and then.

When the girl's owners saw that their hope of gain had gone, they seized Paul and Silas and dragged them to the city authorities in the main square; and bringing them before the magistrates, they said, "These men are causing a disturbance in our city; they are Jews; they are advocating customs which it is illegal for us Romans to adopt and follow." The mob joined in the attack; and the magistrates tore off the prisoners clothes and ordered them to be

12

flogged. After giving them a serve beating they flung them into prison and ordered the jailer to keep them under close guard. Acts 16:16-23, NEB.

That is the first century. Evidently missionary work was having an impact, perhaps on a small scale, but a real impact on the relationships between slaves and slaveowners, what we would call today "exploitation." We can see the consequent reaction of the exploiters. Here, as in the similar story about Ephesus in Acts 19, it is amazing to realize how the arguments against Paul are coined in phrases with a definite political color, appealing to the nationalism of the citizens. Although more evident in Ephesus, there is an ideological construction in both cases. Let us keep this story in mind as a background for our discussion of the issue.

The second story comes from my own country, Peru, not more than two decades ago. It is in one of the novels of the best known Peruvian novelist, Mario Vargas Llosa, entitled *La Casa Verde (The Green House)*. This book is a tragically colorful mosaic that reflects the contradictions of Peruvian society—a semi-feudal structure spread through jungle, highlands, and coast, three clearly different regions. The green house is really a brothel on the northern coast, and the book is a kind of legend built around it. One of the characters is a girl whose childhood in the deep Amazonian jungle is described with masterful strokes; she becomes the object of missionary work that takes her to the mission school and civilization. Then we follow her trip through the highlands to the coast where she finally is involved in the drama of the green house.

Vargas Llosa was asked to tell the story of how he came

13

to write *La Casa Verde* and he has told it in a little booklet which is a nice piece about historical and literary research, Historia Secreta de una Novela (Secret History of a Novel).[2] Here we are told how he gathered the data and became acquainted with the primary material for his characters. As a young university graduate he was invited to visit the Peruvian jungle. Wycliffe Bible translators provided transportation for him. With a couple of professors and a well-known anthropologist he visited several places, including Santa Maria de Nieva. There he met some Spanish nuns who had been working in the area for decades. Vargas Llosa describes how these women who had come from Spain as young girls had immersed themselves in the Peruvian jungle, adapting to life there, literally spending their lives, wearing on their faces the marks of the tough and inclement weather. The author was deeply moved as he saw their sacrificial work.

He continues with a description of their missionary methodology. Police were called to help round up the children whose parents refused to send them to the mission school. Every year there was a hunting excursion to gather them up and bring them to the Roman Catholic religion and civilization. Once they had been civilized the girls would not want to return to their tribe. So the nuns with the help of their acquaintances on the coast—military personnel from the jungle garrisons, businessmen and salesmen who toured the area, civil servants, and so on—usually sent the girls to the coast as maids. The drama of adaptation to a hostile society and environment in the cities pushed some of these girls eventually into the trap of prostitution in the "casas verdes" of the coastal cities.

There is a certain tension in Vargas Llosa's account of

his encounter with missionary work. On the one hand he displays a sense of admiration for the sacrificial work these nuns had been doing there for decades—their dedication to the mission and the heroic nature of their immersion in the jungle. On the other hand the writer was following the course of missionary action beyond the point where the nuns detached themselves from it. He tries to see in perspective what happened to these girls who had been the "fruit" of missionary work. And he has communicated forcefully the ambiguity of the process that began at the mission school and ended at *la casa verde*.

There are many comments we could make at this point. We could say, for instance, that from the viewpoint of civilization to live in *la casa verde* is perhaps far better than to remain in the jungle as an idolater. Whatever we say, as we follow, from a historical and denominational distance, these missionary processes at Philippi and Peru, we have to admit the ambiguities of this relationship between missions, social structures, and social justice.

A Renewed Historical Awareness

To articulate what the missionary task should be in general, and not only in relation to our subject, we need the historical awareness that comes from distance, from a contemplation of the missionary task that grasps its totality—a kind of bird's-eye view—wherever we have the necessary distance and knowledge of the facts to do it. This historical awareness is forced upon us by factors which are internal and external to the life of the church.

One *internal factor* would be, of course, the logical demands of our theology of missions if it has biblical revelation as its starting point. Provisionally I am here equating mission with the numerical and geographical expansion of the church, though I expect to come later to a correction of that equation. Thus we must ask how the missionary task was accomplished by Jesus and by the primitive Christian community in the time span of more or less seventy years that is recorded in the Bible. How did the process take place? How do we understand it? If this pattern is normative at all, we can benefit from the vantage point of nineteen centuries of distance when we contemplate it.

Much research has been done on the subject. We are familiar with the works of Roland Allen and Henry Venn.[3] I would like to mention two recent additions to the research that have caught my attention in a special way. Both concentrate on the biblical material and reflect about it from a definite missiological stance.

Michael Green is himself an evangelist and a pastor, as well as a New Testament scholar. His book *Evangelism in the Early Church*[4] combines research on the life and institutions of societies in the Mediterranean world during the first century with a deep probing into the contents of the Christian message, and the way these two elements interact through the life and advance of the early church. Green was asked to present a paper for the Lausanne Congress on Evangelization (1975), and his initial presentation was criticized for not stressing enough or expounding the "strategy" of the early church's missionary advance. Green's answer from the background of his research and practice was that the apostolic church did not seem to have a blueprint for action in the way in which the contemporary "engineering of missions" demands. In fact, some key advances of the

16

church seem to have happened without planning, becoming a surprise for the apostolic team. What we find in the early church is a clear awareness of and faithfulness to the truth of the living Christ, understood in the rich context of the apostolic kerygma, and an openness to the promptings of the Spirit which was not necessarily perceived in all its dimensions by the early church, and I would add that it is not entirely available to our own perception today.[5]

Jean Paul Audet is a Canadian missiologist who in a small but seminal book, *The Gospel Project*[6], has outlined in a fresh way the missionary project of Jesus Himself. Audet insists on the intentionality of Jesus' choices of stages, models, and preaching emphases. At the initial stage of proclamation Jesus uses for Him and His envoys the Old Testament model of the herald, a swift, mobile, almost ascetic style. Then comes the second stage of consolidation where the model is the teacher and the style becomes didactic, meditative, located in more stable situations. Audet insists on the need to conform our missionary and pastoral practice to those biblical patterns rather than reading our modern patterns back into the text.

What is common to these two missiological reflections on the biblical material is a conviction about the originality of the biblical models, the close relation they have with the nature of biblical truth, and the corrective power they contain for our modern understanding and practice of mission.

An *external factor* that forces historical awareness upon us is the new world situation, especially the postcolonial nature of our times.[7] Without making any value judgement about it we have to assume the fact that today's world is very different from what it was at the beginning of our century, or at the time when missionary fervor was at its height. I insist that we do not need to make any value judgement about the process at this point. We have to acknowledge its existence. Leslie T. Lyall has expressed it this way:

> At the historic world wide missionary conference held in Edinburgh in 1910, in the hey day of Western colonial expansion and before the first of two tragic world wars had shattered the imperial dream, missionary statesmen looked out from their Christian citadel in the West over the pagan world—but a world which their optimism expected soon to become Christian through the influence of Christian colonization in Asia and Africa. They ignored Latin America which many of them regarded as already Christian. In Europe and North America the Church in the Edwardian era was at the height of its power and popularity. Elsewhere in the world it was considered scarcely to exist. The church therefore clearly saw it to be the white Christian's burden to evangelize the heathen and to extend the frontiers of the Christian duty to go further and to include spreading Western or Christian civilization with the Gospel. Sixty years later the picture is profoundly different. The imperial dream has been finally shattered. Imperialism and colonialism instead of proving to be allies of evangelism, came to be regarded after the second world war as its enemies. The church in the Third World is today acutely embarrassed by any past association with either and is trying to live down and outlive the commonly held view that Christianity was in some way a part of the imperialist plot to dominate the world—the spearhead of cultural imperialism.[8]

When from the vantage point of this postcolonial situation we look at the missionary process as it has developed in the last two centuries, we have already a perspective of the results of this missionary action, of the effects it had on history, society, and culture, of the surprises that missionary strategists of the past would have if they could look at the outcome of their projects. All that is part of a renewed historical awareness.

Historical Awareness and Social Justice

We will bring now the same kind of perspective and analysis to the specific area of missions and social justice. Here we are faced with very embarrassing questions and as we try to answer them history may come to our help. Let us start by accepting the fact that the church, even in her most conservative segments in the West, has been led to accept the postcolonial situation with much embarrassment for her past association with colonialism. Here a value judgment about the new historical developments is implied. *This new situation is accepted and recognized as good.* Who would say today that the colonial situation was better than the present one? Have you ever read or heard that opinion in missionary circles? In any missionary literature it is taken for granted that what we have today is better than what we had yesterday. This value judgement is important and it conditions our approach to the subject. But some of the ambiguities come precisely from it.

Again we will consider two kinds of factors—an external one and an internal one, forcing us to historical awareness. The *internal factor* is related to the content of the Christian faith itself and to the imperative it imposes on us in the realm of concern for justice in society. Fresh reflection and exposition of the biblical material comes from at least two sources that I will mention here. One is the renewal of Anabaptist theology of which John

19

Howard Yoder is the most articulate exponent in *The Politics of Jesus.*[9] The other is the creative work of Jacques Ellul, a French sociologist of Reformed extraction. What we have in both cases is an emphasis on the uniqueness of the content of the Christian message to shape a social ethics, i. e., an approach to social problems which is faithful to the thrust of the Biblical message, the example of Christ, and the testimony of the Spirit through the Christian community.

In *The Politics of Jesus* what is detected and expounded is a fresh understanding of the social institutions of the world in New Testament times, and a correction of the notion that what we have in the ethical teaching of the New Testament is nothing but a reflection of that world. Actually Yoder argues that we are confronted in the Bible with something unique and radically different, because it is rooted in the uniqueness of Christian revelation and the history of God's people. This is especially evident in the chapter on "Revolutionary Subordination" where Yoder argues against the commonly held view that Paul's advice to the slaves is mere reflection of Stoic ethics at the service of the status quo.[10]

Several of Ellul's books could be quoted here outlining his contribution to the debate, but I want to mention two that are especially relevant: *Violence: Reflections from a Christian Perspective*[11], and, in Spanish, *El Dinero.*[12] In the first of these Ellul delves into post-apostolic history of Christian attitudes toward violence, but he pushed the analysis back to the example of Jesus Himself as relevant for our time, and argues lucidly for his case. In the second Ellul stresses the element of personal responsibility that the Bible teaches in relation to money, as well as the demonic dimensions that it can take. He warns especially against the recurrent bias to justify and explain Christian behavior by a rationale that accepts the determinism of man by systems.

In both of these cases the strength of the argument lies in the uniqueness of the Christian revelation and warns us against jumping on the bandwagon of any modern ideology as if there were no other ground on which to approach the problem of justice in society. But at the same time and by the same token the discovery of the biblical imperatives becomes a corrective of the easy jump into conformism that the church has frequently adopted.

The *external factor* in the postcolonial situation is the challenge this situation poses to Christians in order to understand that some of the good and desirable situations and elements of the new situation were already present, as a latent force contained in the missionary impulse, message, and action. Anglo-Saxon missiology has been uncovering the facts and we can only mention some of the many pieces of research on the subject. Max Warren in his book *Social History and Christian Mission*[13], analyzes particularly the missionary movement coming out of Britain and the way in which it prepared and developed, in the colonies of Asia and Africa, a middle class which became a factor of change in the independence period. Warren admits openly that the picture is not clear and is surrounded by ambiguities but his careful research has to be taken into account by those who want to talk *responsibly* about colonial and postcolonial realities. (And they are not legion unfortunately.)

A wider scope but a more schematic approach characterizes Norman Goodall's *Christian Mission and Social Ferment*.[14] All through this seminal work we see how varied were the ways in which, consciously or uncon-

21

sciously, Christian missions during the last two centuries prepared the way for the independence and the postcolonial situations.

> The primary object of all this missionary experimentation was the individual, not the social order. The most persistent motive was concern for the person. But the necessity which compelled the "interference" was itself part of an inescapable involvement in society.[15]

Goodall quotes someone saying that in China "the revolution really began when Robert Morrison landed on Chinese soil," thus linking Mao Tse-tung with the first Protestant missionary to China via Sun Yat-sen.

From a different angle Lesslie Newbigin has applied to his missiological reflection the thesis of van Leeuwen about the secularizing force of the Christian message. In *Honest Religion for Secular Man*[16] there is an outline of the process by which the sacral societies in Asia and Africa were open to the processes of development and liberation by the preaching of the biblical message. In this as in other books Newbigin develops a convincing apologetics for missions which by its very articulation enables him to dialogue with men of other faiths.[17]

The concern common to the three missiologists we have just quoted is to see the totality of a historical process in order to perceive how missionary action has penetrated and modified social structures, in a movement that can definitely be qualified as conducive to social justice. We will now turn our attention for a moment to another missiologist who operates with categories that we could describe as totally different from the previous three. Donald McGavran has avowedly made numerical growth of the Christian community the only legitimate category by which he evaluates missionary action. However, the issues related to social justice come across his path with the persistence of historical reality. Let us remember also that though this school of thought eliminates from missionary action all intentions in the direction of social justice, it is at the same time very vocal about the need to understand the social structure inside which the missionary work takes place. How is historical awareness present in McGavran's thought? In his magnum opus *Understanding Church Growth*[18], important material on the subject comes under the title "The Masses, The Classes and Church Growth." This is what he says:

> More than any previous century, ours is conscious of "the masses" and their claim to justice and equality of opportunity. The burden-bearers have always comprised the major part of society, but in the twentieth century they have gained more and more power. Industrialism has created a huge proletariat in our ever enlarging cities. Labour organizations have achieved tremendous strength. The churches have called for social justice. An awakened conscience among national leaders has changed our tax structure in the direction of a more just distribution of wealth. Communism has established dictatorships of the proletariat in many nations, defending these as a necessary step towards a just society. . . . That mankind should be divided into beneficiaries and victims of the social order no longer seems right to thoughtful men. The condition of the disinherited has become a matter of profound concern to the state. Those who fight Communism do so not on the basis that its championing of the masses is wrong, but that it is ineffective, its means and consequences are self-defeating.[19]

It is clearly taken for granted that this postcolonial situation, in which the role of the masses is recognized as different and the common man is respected, is better than the previous situation. A value judgement has been passed. McGavran, however, goes beyond that point and proposes a missionary methodology that takes seriously the situation and operates accordingly. At no point does he suggest that it would be desirable to return to an aristocratic view of society instead of the current populism. At several points in the rest of this book we will deal critically with the contradictions of the strategy he proposes but let us keep in mind the acceptance of the new situation on his part.

Applying the Concept: the Case of John Wesley

If our observations up to this point give us some degree of historical awareness we are better prepared to understand the relationship between Christian mission and social justice. Such understanding is especially necessary in our time because due to historical acceleration or to the deep penetration of revolutionary ideologies the notion of social justice tends to be linked to the notion of rapid change or revolution. Because of this tendency it is not easy to trace the courage of the forces that foster or produce social justice. This course is ambiguous and lends itself to misunderstanding. Its direction can only be traced by following phenomena in their long duration of centuries and in the multifaceted complexity of its human components. There is always the danger of oversimplification, and short-circuiting of action as a consequence.

What we are trying to say can be better grasped from an eloquent example taken from the well-known British historian Gordon Rupp. In his book *Principalities and Powers* Rupp gives us a provocative collection of "studies in the Christian conflict in history" which combine biblical conviction with an enviable familiarity with the factual stuff of European and British history. The great themes of biblical history, eschatology, and grace are expounded and illustrated with vivid examples of their contemporaneity. He establishes a clear contrast between the "pessimism of grace" in Catholic and Protestant divines of the seventeenth century, and the "optimism of nature" characteristic of the rationalist philosophers of the eighteenth and nineteenth centuries. But he also uncovers for us a totally different element from Wesley's "Evangelical Arminianism" that could be characterized as "an optimism of grace." In that context Rupp asks a question that is relevant to our subject and answers it in a way that can better be enjoyed from the long quotation that it demands:

Propaganda history oversimplifies and foreshortens. The statement has often been made that John Wesley and the Evangelical Revival saved England from a French Revolution. That played right into the hands of the left-wing historians who have long criticized Methodism for a pietism which was opium of the people. Grace works in and through history, but it takes time for the gospel to penetrate the social and political levels of any culture. The question why the Gordon riots in London in 1780 did not develop into national revolution, and why the Chartist's march on London in 1848 broke under the strain of the English secret weapon, an all-day shower of rain, is complex, but the answer lies very far back. I would almost venture the half-truth: not John Wesley but Henry VIII saved England from a French Revolution; not the Evangelical Revival but the wars of the Roses decisively and profoundly affected the class structure of the English people. And if I had to single out a deep religious impulse in the differentiation among England, France and Germany, I would give the credit to seventeenth-century Puritanism that English life did not collapse in 1789. That is not at all to deny the profound political and social repercussions of Methodism to which I have paid tribute above. If John Wesley did not save us in 1789, he may have saved us in 1848, or even in 1940. I am not trying to make a point in the somewhat spinsterish way in which church historians politely cut one another's throats, but to utter a warning to those who speak rather too easily about Christianity saving civilization, and use the phrase as a threat and as a promise in evangelistic, religious or political speeches. We easily give the impression that some vast conjuring trick is within our grasp. Yet if a revival of religion began today, bigger and more effective than all previous revivals of Christianity put together, it would still leave untouched a great part of humanity, and still greater areas of human life untouched as yet by the Christian spirit.[20]

Both in our grasp of history and in the application of its lessons to our missiology we must remember the warning against short-circuiting and the awareness of distance and duration. There is the temptation to believe that a simplified and cursory reading of history enables us to re-produce some processes of the past and that temptation is especially attractive in the area of social justice.

Applying the Concept: Latin American Protestantism

Another historical instance which is clarified by ap-plication of this notion of historical awareness is that of the social impact of Latin American Protestantism. The ambiguities of the process can become dramatic for us because we live in situations directly linked with this process, and we minister inside circumstances derived from it. We cannot use the term "Latin American Protestantism" unequivocally, without mentioning the variety of origins, composition, and style that char-

so-called faith missions. We would not exaggerate if we say that groups that preach the new birth and demand a commitment that implies breaking away from the Roman Catholic Church are automatically described as "sects" even by avowed ecumenists. And it does have a derogatory meaning in socio-theological usage.

Is Vallier's statement true? I think that we can answer positively. Let me clarify that I am not thinking about the assistance work of Protestantism which in itself is a very important chapter of its history and should not be overlooked or underestimated. It is a fact for instance, that the school system that the Methodists and Presbyterians brought to Latin America had a double impact. On the one hand it counteracted the monopoly of education for certain social classes that the Roman Church exerted. It was also an incentive to the state to change its own educational system. My positive answer has to do with the impact of Protestantism in the social structures, in the direction of social justice. What do we find there?

Protestantism was a factor of change and the impulse and dynamic for its impact came from its Anabaptist stance. Until 1933 in a country like Peru you could not prove your identity unless you were ready to either be baptized in the Roman church or go through a complicated legal process. Or again, in Argentina, the fight for religious freedom that was going to affect not only Protestants but also Jews and others was fought in the initial decades of our century. By their simple existence Protestants were forcing a change in society. By their persistence in their loyalty to a faith different than the official creed, they were challenging an unjust structure. Thus even pietistic groups with no clear political conscience or intention had in their ranks brave pioneers of social freedom like the Swiss pastor Pablo Besson in Argentina or the Scottish layman and missionary John Ritchie in Peru. Their activities reached even the parliament of these nations. This also explains why modernizing forces in these societies looked to the Protestants with sympathy and hope. Presidents like Domingo F. Sarmiento in Argentina, Eloy Alfaro in Ecuador, and Benito Juárez in Mexico were vocal in their preference for Protestant presence and influence in their countries, even though they did not become Protestant themselves. During the first three decades of our century, the modernizing forces that wanted to change the old structures of society welcomed the presence of Protestantism and Protestant missions. There has been no serious study of that phenomenon, but the primary sources are there waiting for a scholar to uncover and interpret.[23]

It is important to remember that at that point in history North America had become the ideal model for the modernizing forces—so much so that Jose Enrique Rodo, the great Uruguayan thinker, wrote a book that criticized the search for an Anglo-Saxon model that stressed the pragmatic, activist, and—for him—materialistic concept of life. *Ariel* and the movement that took its name was a reaction against this search for modernity. It was not a reaction in the name of feudalism and Catholicism, but more the expression of an elitist European-oriented humanism. However, among those segments of society that were in a process of transition—from rural to urban, for instance—Protestantism grew at a great speed. The success of the ministry of a man like John A. Mackay among students and intellectuals was also an evidence of openness to an expression of Christianity different from the feudalistic Catholicism that was official. However, this did not give birth to the appearance of a Protestant intelligentsia. The real growth of Protestantism happened among the masses. This takes us to a final reflection.

Contemporary Loss of Vigor

If we recognize that an open pluralistic society, where a minority such as Protestants or Jews can exist without being discriminated against or forced to conversion, is a better society and a more just society, we have to acknowledge also the positive role toward social justice that Protestant missionary work played in the period here considered (1850-1950). We have some distance now to see the process and appreciate its results. Precisely that perspective can also help us to understand better the role of Protestantism today and the degree to which it has kept its social dynamism in the Latin American situation. Let us keep in mind that there was not always a concerted effort to change society among the missionaries who went to Latin America with the gospel. What made them a force for change was faithfulness to their understanding of the biblical gospel, courage to stand for it facing a hostile society and persecution, and awareness of the levels of society at which dialogue and negotiation were necessary to foster change.

The other factor that we have to keep in mind is that from a sociological viewpoint Protestantism tended to produce an upward mobility. This can be seen in the growth and development of several denominations. Having started work at the lower levels of the social scale, in a matter of one or two generations we find these communities in the middle class. Most of the non-Pentecostal denominations today are typically middle class in their value system, social preferences, attitude toward society, goals in life, and social role. And it seems that their social position has stifled their social dynamism, their concern for social justice, and their possibilities of providing any light in a society that faces dramatic alternatives.

A helpful observation on this matter comes from Charles Denton, himself a Protestant, born in Latin America, and a sociologist specialized in Latin American affairs. He first observes the need to recognize that the Latin American middle classes are not playing the dynamic role the middle class has played in other societies.

Latin American social scientists in particular have questioned the benefits of a rising middle class in their countries. . . . They question the attitudes and behaviour of the Latin American middle classes. Nun, Veliz, Ratinoff, Adams and a growing group of Latin American specialists from various disciplines have noted that if a middle class does exist in the area, it is the least democratic and socially conscious group in any of the countries. Rather than striking out for moderation and stability, it is the middle class which is responsible for the military insurrections which have ocurred at an alarming rate since 1959 after a period in the 50's when it appeared that militarism was on the wane in Latin America. The Latin American middle class rather than striving for an identity of its own, has chosen to imitate, even to ape the more traditional upper classes in attitude, dress, behaviour, and in every possible aspect of their lives. This situation reveals itself in a thousand different ways, from the scorn of a poorly paid clerk in a government office toward those who work with their hands to voting behaviour. Because members of the middle class are in a more precarious position, socially and economically, than their upper class mentors, the tendency has been for the former to be even more distrustful of change, reform, or anything else that might affect their position than the latter.[24]

What has happened to the Protestantism that has arrived into this class? What has been the effect of the heritage of social dynamism that it had at its initial stages? Moreover, how have the biblical values and teachings affected the arrival of Protestants in this environment?

Denton points out the many missiological and pastoral problems derived from the already mentioned social mobility that Protestantism generates. He says further:

> A second major problem is the fact that as Protestants do enter the middle class they are becoming too well integrated. Rather than becoming a force for new standards of efficiency and for reform they have usually adopted the socio-economic norms of their new peer group as described above. . . . From the perspective of the reformist-oriented Latin American intellectual, the Protestant movement is regarded as contributing to the status quo of the country or countries. In some quarters it is even heard that the Protestant movement is a fifth column for United States imperialism in Latin America.[25]

The illustrations that Denton uses to prove his point are in the realm of attitudes toward work, manual labor, lower classes, and emphasis on the external and formal acts of religion as status symbols, all of which reflect middle class rather than biblical standards.

Probably this phenomenon explains the unqualified support, even adulation, given by vocal Protestant segments to the military regimes that overthrew populist governments in countries like Brazil and Chile. The final outcome of these present historical roles that Protestants are playing, is yet to be seen but it is evident that by comparison we can see that we have entered into the realm of ambiguity in missionary work and its fruits as we see them in historical perspective. There is a loss of dynamism in relation to the change of society, an accommodation to sociological pressures, and a lack of coherence between the biblical creed and behavior in the community. It has to be recognized that some aspects of the present process may be explained by the fact that the more vocal and active force for social change happens to be Marxism in our continent these days, and that being avowedly anti-Christian it may have produced in the Protestant community a fear of change, justified in view of the fate of Christian churches in countries where Marxism is the official religion. My contention is that this position is not taken by Protestants today on the basis of the Christian message itself or the historical experience of the church. It has rather become an identification with the-world-as-it-stands.

It is at this point also that I can come back to my criticism of Donald McGavran and his missiology. Though he has words of approval for the nationalist leaders in Korea and the Phillippines during the 1920s, and for the role that Christianity played positively toward social justice at that point,[26] his insistence on a numerical growth linked to a preaching of a minimum of the gospel and at the expense of reflection and criticism of the role of the church is producing a missiology of accommodation that will produce communities that will not have the dynamism that comes from the totality of biblical truth and the self awareness of the Christian community in the light of that truth. His missiology does not take seriously into account the challenges to our faith posed by nationalists in the 1970s. By its lack of historical awareness it is also a missiology that tends to propagate a truncated form of Christianity.

What we have tried to say in this chapter can be summarized in three points. *First,* we need historical distance in order to understand the nature of the relationship between missions and social justice. *Second,* our perception of our own times, as well as that of past historical processes, shows clear ambiguities in this relationship. *Third,* two factors force us into definitions that may shape our obedience to Christ today: the imperatives of our message itself and the external conditions that surround missionary work as it develops now. From this starting point we will examine in the next two chapters several specific areas of our subject: the gospel and the poor, and the dilemma between reform and revolution.

Notes

1. *The Future of the Missionary Enterprise,* a report from IDOC International, number 9, "In Search of Mission" (Rome, 1974), p. 74.

2. Mario Vargas Llosa, *La Casa Verde* (Barcelona: Ed. Seix Barral, 1967) and *Historia Secreta de una Novela* (Barcelona: Ed. Tusquets, 1971).

3. There is a good summary of these studies in Wilbert R. Shenk, "Church Growth Studies," in Wilbert R. Shenk, ed., *The Challenge of Church Growth* (Scottdale: Herald Press, 1973), pp. 7-9. See also Shenk's *Bibliography of Henry Venn's Printed Writings with Index* (Scottdale: Herald Press, 1975).

4. Michael Green, *Evangelism in the Early Church* (London: Hodder and Soughton, 1970).

5. See Michael Green, "Methods and Strategy in the Evangelism of the Early Church," and "Evangelism in the Early Church," in J. D. Douglas, ed., *Let the Earth Hear His Voice* (Minneapolis: World Wide Publications) pp. 159-180, especially pp. 174-175.

6. Jean Paul Audet, *The Gospel Project* (New York: Paulist Press, 1972).

7. A brief but excellent model for analysis of this situation can be

found in Wilbert R. Shenk, "Missions in Retrospect and Prospect," *Christianity Today* (July 28, 1972), pp. 8-12.

8. Leslie T. Lyall, *A World to Win* (London: Inter-Varsity Press— Overseas Missionary Fellowship, 1972). p. 27.

9. John Howard Yoder, *The Politics of Jesus* (Grand Rapids: Eerdmans, 1972).

10. *Ibid.*, pp. 163-192.

11. Jacques Ellul, *Violence: Reflections from a Christian Perspective* (New York: Seabury Press, 1969).

12. Jacques Ellul, *El Dinero* (Valencia: Fomento de Cultura, 1962). [*L'Homme et l'Argent* (Paris and Neuchatel: Delachaux et Niestle, 1954)].

13. Max Warren, *Social History and Christian Mission* (London: SCM Press, 1967).

14. Norman Goodall, *Christian Mission and Social Ferment* (London: Epworth Press, 1964).

15. *Ibid.*, p. 20.

16. Lesslie Newbigin, *Honest Religion for Secular Man* (London: SCM Press, 1966).

17. Lesslie Newbigin, *A Faith for This One World* (London: SCM Press, 1962).

18. Donald McGavran, *Understanding Church Growth* (Grand Rapids: Eerdmans, 1970).

19. *Ibid.*, p. 235.

20. E. Gordon Rupp, *Principalities and Powers* (Epworth: Wyvern Books, 1963), pp. 88-89.

21. I have also developed this reflection in "El Reino de Dios, la Escatologia y la Etica Social y Politica en America Latina," in C. Rene Padilla, ed., *El Reino de Dios y America Latina* (El Paso: Casa Bautista de Publicaciones, 1975).

22. Ivan Vallier, *Catholicism, Social Control and Modernization in Latin America* (Englewood Cliffs: Prentice-Hall, 1970), pp. 58-59.

23. An essay of interpretation that follows closely a Marxist approach to the issue is presented by Jose Miguez Bonino, *Doing Theology in a Revolutionary Situation* (Philadelphia: Fortress Press, 1975), pp. 10-20.

24. Charles F. Denton, "Protestantism and the Latin American Middle Class," *Practical Anthropology* (Jan-Feb 1971), p. 25.

25. *Ibid.*, p. 27.

26. McGavran, *op.cit.*, pp. 221-223 and 235-259.

2

The Gospel and the Poor

Samuel Escobar

There is a new awareness of poverty in the world today which affects missionary action in a special way. Our situation in relation to poverty is in open contrast to that of the primitive church, because in New Testament days the gospel's advance went from a poor, underdeveloped part of the world to the metropolis of the empire. The problem of the missionary representing a higher standard of living or a more sophisticated kind of cultural achievement and technological progress did not exist. Contrary-wise, younger churches had a feeling of paying a debt to the mother church in Jerusalem when they could send her an offering for her financial problems. This factor should not be overlooked in our effort to find biblical standards for our missionary practice. The affluence of the "sending" churches today as they go from a Christendom situation to poor and primitive or impoverished lands is a new element qualitatively distinct from the situation of the primitive church.

A New Awareness of Poverty in the World

Two aspects of the new awareness of poverty in our contemporary situation are especially significant for our subject. The first involves the conviction that poverty in one part of the world is related to affluence in the other part. The second, more specifically related to missions, is that the gospel is announced to the poor and that the churches grow especially among the poor.

The first conviction has been very aptly expressed by the late president Salvador Allende of Chile who stated in a famous speech to the twenty-seventh session of the United Nations: "Underdevelopment exists because imperialism exists, and imperialism exists because underdevelopment exists." He was expressing what Dennis Goulet describes:

> Buried deep in the consciousness of the Third World masses is the conviction that poverty is the by-product of wealth, the fruit of exploitation and injustice.[1]

Let me call your attention to the fact that behind this consciousness of an interrelation between the poverty of some and the affluence of others, there are some basic presuppositions that we cannot easily dismiss, which we as Christians must evaluate for their significance. One is *the notion of a universal history* that now is almost universally accepted. This concept has not always been grasped and accepted by mankind. Those acquainted with the philosophy of history know that this is a unique

Judeo-Christian contribution to the world which has found acceptance after a long and interesting process. This new awareness, forced into our view of the world by facts such as the progress of communications and the growing interrelatedness of national histories, is something about which Christians can rejoice.

The other presupposition is that poverty is no longer accepted passively as the result of a "distributive justice" of God that gives much to some and little to others. People are no longer "content" with poverty, and there are several reasons for that. Think, for instance, of this description of a Latin American situation:

> It is not only that sixteen-year-old Latin Americans of this land weigh ninety-five pounds and are five feet tall; the point is that at the other side of the avenue he can see other boys the same age who are six feet six and weigh one hundred and twenty-six pounds. It is not just that they will hardly live to see their grandchildren, their life expectancy being way below forty. They know that disease and death can be pushed back and the joys of life can be enjoyed twenty years more. Rapid and luxurious cars, TV sets, new dresses, fun and comfort are displayed everywhere, and even backwoods populations can see them in the newspapers in which their miserable purchases are wrapped. Commercials and political propaganda, Sears Roebuck catalogues and Communist pamphlets produce the same results. The eyes of the poor are transfixed by the picture of this heaven he must obtain at all costs. Life without it is intolerable. This is the revolutionary temper, this is the face of the Latin American and of the whole underdeveloped world—a face contorted by hunger, expectation and wrath. This is the face of revolutionary man.[2]

Poverty and wealth are not accepted anymore as a kind of natural order, and with rising expectations has come an awareness that these differences are man-made differences that have developed in the process of history. The concept of a divine hand behind the economic process, giving much to those who worked hard and deserve the fruit of their labors, is being questioned.

It is important to remember that the general atmosphere out of which the modern missionary movement came accepted almost without question the idea of a distributive justice that operated in both interclass and international relations. It was even thought that missions were going to help in the process of enlightenment so that the underdeveloped would raise themselves to the level of the so-called Christian nations. The new element in the awareness of poverty is that there is after all no desire on the part of the wealthy nations to raise the poor nations because raising the poor would endanger their own wealth and undermine their power. Missions from the developed nations have to take this new awareness very seriously. Poverty is no longer a simple datum that you consider neutrally. Missions have to do something about it. After all, they could be part of the system that produces poverty or maintains it.

Good News to the Poor

The second conviction that we mentioned comes from the observation of the history of missions. It seems that in a literal sense, the gospel is announced to the poor and that the church grows more among the poor. This has become one of the strong emphases of some missiological schools of thought. It seems that it is just the poor who are open to the gospel and accept it. One senses a kind of cynicism about this fact behind some arguments, as if the strategy might be: "Better leave people poor so that they
39

remain open to the gospel." Not long ago I participated in an ecclesiastical gathering with my friend Dr. David Gomez from Brazil. He said to a group of American churchmen: "Send us more missionaries soon. In Brazil we are soon going to become a developed nation. Soon there will be no poverty in my fatherland, and there will be no more opportunity for the preaching of the gospel." I discussed this with him and it was evident that he meant what he said: poverty is a condition in which the heart is open to the gospel.

As we look at the growth of Christian communities today, where do we see churches growing? Where is there extension and advance? Among the poor, definitely. The growth of Pentecostalism in Latin America is the growth of a church of the poor. The church life, liturgy, and structures presuppose a situation of poverty as a starting point, even if it is true that conversion produces an upward mobility.

Here we must pause in order to consider history. One fact must be accepted here. *The world is indebted to Christian missions for the uplifting of the poor.* We should not let this fact be obscured by our modern approach to the subject. Modern criticism of the links between imperialism and missions in the immediate past, however valid, should not close our eyes to the fact that missionaries went to the poor and in many cases identified with them in unique and prophetic ways. Let me mention an example. We are all familiar with the call for a moratorium on missionary finances and personnel that has become known especially through the now famous address that Reverend John Gatu presented to the Reformed Church in the America Missions Festival. In that call Gatu mentioned a phrase from David Livingstone's address to his home board, a phrase that has been quoted innumerable times: "I go back to Africa to try to make an open path for commerce and Christianity." Reverend Gatu's comment is well taken: "You must note the sequence, commerce and Christianity."[3] However, I would like to quote Livingstone in a different context. In one of his enlightening *CMS News-letters* John V. Taylor gives us a review of recent studies about Livingstone against the background of modern Africa which includes the following:

> Livingstone the missionary, and Livingstone the champion of African freedom, would be no less delighted than astonished at the situation in Africa today. Dr. A. C. Ross the historian . . . (has) recalled that shortly after Livingstone's home station and most of his possessions had been destroyed by Boer commandos as a reprisal for his support of the Bakwena people, he wrote in a letter to the London Missionary Society: "Everywhere there is a strong feeling of independence springing up. The English, as a nation, have lost character and honour. The destruction of my property is a fortunate thing for me. There is not a native in the country but knows now for certain on whose side I am."[4]

That was also Livingstone! And that is also an important part of missionary history to which we have to do justice: Not only a presence among the poor, but an *alignment* with the poor with the consequent risks and interferences.

Interference with the Secular

With this expression Goodall refers to another form of presence and alignment with the poor that took missionaries to an open interference in the secular affairs of the communities where they worked. They went beyond

41

simple assistance, and a careful consideration of the available literature shows that their motivation was not the imposition of a European or Western model of social organization but a humane and compassionate consideration both out of biblical convictions. Goodall considers, for example, the work of Christian missions in the South Seas and comes to the conclusion that their impact "resulted in a radical reshaping of the social pattern." Missionaries from the London Missionary Society and the Methodist Missionary Society working in Tahiti were active in creating codes of laws for the converted kings who wanted to shape their small societies according to Christian principles. Some of their efforts may sound naive to us, but that does not make them less valuable and decisive. Thus John Williams included lawmaking among his missionary activities, and helped to institute trial by jury, which for him constituted "the greatest barrier to oppression" and one of the "permanent foundations for the civil liberties" of the people in Cook Island. Horrified by the punishment inflicted by tribal custom even for small offenses, he acted to change it:

> None of these sanguinary modes of punishment were in accordance with the spirit of the merciful religion which the chiefs now professed, and wishing that their civil and judicial policy should be so, they naturally appealed to us for advice. Thus was a necessity laid upon us to act in these affairs; and while we gave the chiefs clearly to understand that our objects were purely of a spiritual character, we were convinced that, under existing circumstances, it was as much a duty to direct them in the formation of a code of laws as it was to instruct them in the principles of Christianity itself, for in thus acting *we were simply advising them to apply those principles to social life and to substitute them for ferocity and revenge.*[5]

This concern for those who could become victims of a cruel system of social punishment is a form of concern for the poor. A critical anthropologist might have preferred to leave the cruel punishments untouched, either for the sake of authenticity in the native culture or for his own benefit as a curious observer of human behavior. Not so the missionary, of course. He interfered on behalf of the poor.

There is another type of action for the poor which, without being a direct interference at the level of power in a society, has an impact that eventually touches the social structure. It can be illustrated by an experience in Bolivia. More than fifty years ago, a missionary group called Peniel Society bought some land in Huatajata, Bolivia, in order to help Aymara peasants with a school and a hospital. As was the practice until recently in Latin America, the land was sold with 250 Aymara serfs who were considered part of the estate. After a period of failures and hesitations, the project was handed over to the Canadian Baptist Mission Board in 1920. An agricultural missionary and other services were brought in, but very little fruit of these efforts was evident. It took a long process to come to the point that Norman Dabbs summarizes:

> It finally dawned on the missionaries that their position as landowners and serf-masters was overriding every benevolent attempt to uplift the people.[6]

Some modern missiologists would have considered that the early attempts were an evidence of a nonreceptive population. The missionaries have bought the land to help them, but they do not come to school or to church. Evidently they are not receptive to the gospel. The cor-

43

respondence between the missionaries and their board shows the varied and discouraging interpretations of the fact. At last comes the conclusion: "Maybe it is because they see us as their masters; we should change our roles and our status in relation to them." In 1942 economic serfdom was abolished, the land was parceled, and the Aymaras were given their titles of property to their plots. Norman Dabbs describes the moving ceremony and concludes: "Both missionaries and peons felt that a crushing weight had been lifted from their lives."

Two other illuminating facts follow this action. Ten years later in 1952, a nationalist revolutionary movement passed the desperately needed law of land reform which changed the economic structure of Bolivia in the direction of a more just society. During the process of change express mention was made of the Huatajata experiment as a valid precedent. The other fact is that after land reform in Huatajata missionary work flourished in a new way, and after land reform in the country the growth of the church among the Aymaras increased dramatically. The charts of church growth statisticians show a definite jump after 1952. About the relationship between missionaries and Indians in Huatajata we can definitely say that it was radically affected by the distribution of the land and the liberation of the servants. Could we also say that the possession of a piece of land brought with itself a new freedom to the Aymaras, and that their economic freedom meant also a freedom to choose a church whose message was redemption? Personally I think that we can establish here a valid correlation.

A Classist Understanding of "The Gospel to the Poor"

Here we come to the complex issue of church growth

in relation to the poor. The idea that the gospel is announced to the poor can be interpreted in curious dimensions. Take for instance the classist interpretation given by a Chilean pastor, Victor Manuel Mora. In 1928 he founded a church to which you could belong only if you were a mine worker and a socialist. It was definitely a church for the poor, moreover a church for the workers of a certain political persuasion, linked to the vision of a given class.[7]

"The gospel to the poor" can also be understood with a classist interpretation in a different way. Many Latin Americans who have a liberal political persuasion have a view that could be summarized as follows: "We the enlightened classes do not need religion. We approve of your preaching to the poor. They need it. For them it is the only basis for good behavior. Protestant religion is good to save them from drunkenness, laziness, sexual promiscuity, and their tendency to steal." I have found more than one American businessman in Latin America who would be skeptical or cynical about the value of the Christian message for himself, but at the same time would be supportive of missionary efforts if they would produce "better natives." Probably these are variations of a position expressed by Nietzsche that Christianity was Platonism for the masses.

Beyond these ways of understanding the relationship between poverty and the gospel, but still closely related to it, is what we could describe as "classist missiology," expressed particularly by Donald McGavran. In a book we have already mentioned, McGavran takes pains to make his readers aware that the masses of the world outside North America and Europe are poor today and that when we think of missions we should turn toward them

45

rather than toward the small upper and middle classes. He realizes that it is no easy task to convince his readers:

> Though they have their poor, Americans are accustomed to a unified society and do not like to speak about "the classes and the masses." The carpenter earns as much as the college teacher and the millworker drives a better car than the minister. The idea of a privileged aristocracy is alien to our national ethos. So while they sometimes talk about the masses, Americans do not really know what it is to live as victims of the social order. In fact we are apt to think "victims of the social order" too barbed a phrase to describe any portion of our society. . . . Notwithstanding this, America has her exploited classes. . . .[8]

McGavran proceeds to demonstrate that a careful reading of the Bible shows a preference of God for the poor. Later in this chapter we will examine this statement. However, McGavran uses it only as the basis for a missionary strategy that will concentrate on the masses rather than the elite, in order to see numerical growth:

> Eurican° Churches are middle-class Churches. Most missionaries are middle-class people. They have grown up with interior plumbing, electric light, and plenty of books. They ride in cars and travel to the lands of their work in jet planes. Really in relation to the masses of the lands to which they go, they are not middle but upper-class people. Naturally they create middle-class Churches. There is nothing surprising in this. . . . But for the most part, the strategy of winning the upper classes first has not worked. They will not be won. The middle classes "have it too good." Why should they risk losing it all to become Christians?[9]

Consequently, if it is among the masses that receptivity is found as statistics demonstrate, the strategy should be to

___

° This neologism means European and North American.

"win the winnable." The concern of this missiology is basically methodological, having defined numerical growth of the churches as its objective.

These three ways of understanding "the gospel to the poor" are not basically questioning poverty nor trying to define the nature of the Christian presence among the poor. Poverty is taken as a datum only in order to define a strategy that has nothing to do with either the impact of the Christian message on the fact of poverty or social change directed to the elimination of poverty. But our interest in this reflection cannot stay at that point. Having seen in sections 2 and 3 some instances of the historical impact of the Christian mission on poverty and the specific nature that the Christian presence took in the past, we must turn our attention now to the biblical material, thus complementing the awareness that will help us to see the present in perspective.

Jesus Among the Poor.

The expression "the gospel to the poor" is an expression that Jesus used precisely in relation to the definition of His own mission (Luke 4:18; 7:22). How did He accomplish this mission of preaching the gospel to the poor? What was the nature of Jesus' presence among the poor? We can only mention some elements that help us in the direction of an answer to these questions, without attempting a deep study of the subject.

The first fact of Jesus' presence among the poor is that it was *the presence of a poor Man among the poor.* Writing to the Corinthians Paul says:

For you know how generous our Lord Jesus Christ has been: he was rich, yet for your sake he became poor, so that

47

through his poverty you might become rich. 2 Corinthians
8:9, NEB.

Interestingly enough, this comment comes in the midst
of a discussion about money in the church. Here, as in
the Christological passage of Philippians 2:4-11, we can
observe how Paul related theological statements to the
daily life of the church. Reading these passages we are
immediately aware of the deep spiritual significance they
have. There is here a reference to the incarnation. "He
was God (rich) and he became man (poor) for our sake."
But let us not forget that in the passage there is more
than that. The fact is that sociologically speaking Jesus
was poor, in the same way in which concretely, historically, He died on a cross.

Gonzalo Baez Camargo, the well-known Mexican
Evangelical, wrote several years ago a moving page
about Jesus, "the proletarian of Nazareth." He reminded
us that Jesus' language and imagery in his teaching could
better be understood by the poor: clothes that have to be
patched, people who cannot afford to loose a coin. Can
affluent people who do not patch clothes anymore grasp
all the force of His statements? This Jesus did not always
know where He was going to spend the night; He had to
ask for a coin in loan in order to illustrate a point. The atmosphere of the Gospels is an atmosphere of poverty; the
communication process there presupposes the experience
of poverty. Yes, Jesus was a poor citizen in a poor
province of the Roman Empire.

This fact has decisive consequences. Take for instance
Jesus' well-known saying, "You have the poor among
you always" (Matthew 26:11 and parallels), which is
frequently quoted to advocate total detachment from

social action or social involvement on behalf of the poor.[10] If we pause to think that these words were pronounced by a poor Man who lived among the poor and spent His life in service which sprang out of compassion for the poor, we can better understand at least what those words *do not mean.* The fact is that usually when used by people who are not poor, the words have a different meaning. They really come to mean, "The rich you will always have with you," because they are used to defend a position that refuses to change things, to be bothered by inequalities and injustices.

Again, when we read Paul's statement, "Poor ourselves, we bring wealth to many; penniless, we own the world" (2 Corinthians 6:10), he is not speaking figuratively; he is describing a fact. As he says, writing to the Philippians, he has learned the freedom of not being conditioned by wealth, of being free in relation to possessions:

> I have been very thoroughly initiated into the human lot with all its ups and downs—fullness and hunger, plenty and want. Philippians 4:12, NEB.

Paul's mission was no doubt possible because of this ability to move freely from the house of a well-to-do businesswoman like Lydia to the depths of a Philippian jail.

The style of Jesus' and Paul's presence among the poor—and for that matter the style of the primitive church also—involves this disposition to enter "into the human lot" to minister to the poor from inside the situation of poverty. This is what modern language calls identification. It is not a paternalistic ministry from the distance of a protected compound. And definitely it has its serious risks: the poor and the downtrodden of society

49

are the ones you find in jail, on crosses. Isn't this the lesson that Livingstone had learned when the Boers burned his mission station? Isn't this the lesson that Canadian Baptists learned in Bolivia when they stopped being the masters of the Aymaras?

A Biblical Understanding of "The Poor"

Up to this point our use of the term "poor" has had a definite sociological content. From our use it can be understood that we have meant dispossession or standing inside a certain segment of society. But when we try to understand the biblical use of the terms translated "poor" in our language we discover a depth and complexity of meaning to which we must turn our attention for a moment. We can take Jesus' statement about the gospel being announced to the poor or the first beatitude as recorded by Matthew, trying to see them in the context of their Old Testament background. Thus we find in the Pentateuch usage of "poor," a content that is basically sociological, especially in the legislation about the poor (Leviticus 25; Deuteronomy 15). In the psalms and the Preexilic prophets, the connotations of piety, goodness, and meekness come to add to our understanding in such a way that sometimes the translators have used, for instance, "meekness" or "poverty" to translate the same Hebrew root, עָכָךְ . In the Postexilic prophets the idea of the remnant is added with all its historical and missionary significance.[11]

So when Jesus states that the gospel is announced to the poor, or when He starts the Beatitudes with the blessedness of the poor, *there is more than a simple sociological reference*. Truly, as we have already argued, the sociological content cannot be eliminated by spiritualization. But neither can the richer spiritual meaning be truncated by sociology.

The gospel of the kingdom is thus announced by Jesus Christ to every man, but there are ears open among those "who know they are poor" (Matthew 5:3). Evidently most of those people seemed to be among those who were also sociologically poor. However we can understand that there is more than a simple sociological reference here. Matthew, Levi, Nicodemus, Joseph of Arimathea were not sociologically poor but they had an open heart to the riches of God that the poor Preacher from Nazareth was bringing. In this they were closer to the sociologically poor of their day, closer to those that were powerless, dispossessed, downtrodden. In the best biblical tradition regardless of their sociological standing, the term "poor" could also be used to describe Simeon and Anna, "upright and devout people who watched and waited for the restoration of Israel and the liberation of Jerusalem" (Luke 2:25-38). This also happens with the apostolic church both in what we know about her practices through the Book of Acts as well as in the teaching about her identity and vocation that we find in the Epistles, especially that of Paul to the Corinthians and that of James.[12]

There is a contemporary trend to equate "the poor" with the modern concept of "class," especially in the theology of liberation by its acceptance of the Marxist analysis of society. A clear expression of this trend is presented by Sergio Rostagno prior to the great diffusion of the Latin American theologians of liberation.[13] This Italian Waldensian analyzes the biblical material, especially in James and Luke, with their Old Testament background and warns us:

51

All these passages indicate that the Christian message would be distorted if it were to be taken as a neutral statement, addressed to men regardless of their times and circumstances. It is obvious, on the other hand, that it would be anachronistic to look for a materialist analysis of history in these texts.[14]

Rostagno also analyzes Paul's teaching to the Corinthians in the first chapter of the first Epistle, relating it to God's action in justification and God's justice. And again, he concludes:

The Jewish ideal, according to which God rewards the good (i.e., the poor) and punishes the wicked (i.e., the rich), could not be accepted by Christianity. And one would have to be rather naive to try at the present time to deduce the class struggle from the Jewish premise in question, as if this is what the class struggle means and as if it could thus be transformed into a sort of "holy war."[15]

In spite of the lucidity of his analysis, however, we cannot agree with the final thesis with which it concludes: "An interclass reading of the Bible is illegitimate." This thesis is followed by others that show some of the presuppositions and consequences of the premise. We quote some of them:

1. An interclass reading of the Bible is illegitimate.
1.1 Both we and the text are conditioned by society.
2.1 We are now in a position to work out scientifically the theory of exploitation and to trace poverty and riches to precise causes. All fatalism is idolatrous especially if professed by Christians.
2.2 Once the causes have been made clear, it is impossible not to try to think out measures for changing the production relationships which result in exploitation. The change has to be undertaken as a human task. It

should not be regarded as the implementation of metaphysical presuppositions.

2.4 The Christian vocation must be worked out in materialistic practice. There is no such thing as a Christian practice which would be the implementation of Christian presuppositions. The Christian reaffirms the complementarity of a practice and a language which make the search for truth possible.[16]

In other words, Rostagno holds that because the church as a community is already divided into classes an interclass reading of the Bible is not possible. A previous alignment is posed with an almost deterministic character. Not only that, but it is denied that there exists a unique Christian way of being among the poor. Having in mind the elements of Christian history as well as the content of the message and its normative character for us today we cannot accept Rostagno's thesis. In fact our suspicion is that his reading of the biblical material starts with an alignment and a way of reading Christian history that is imposed on reality as can be seen from this initial paragraph of the article we are mentioning:

Historically speaking the church has always been a Church of the bourgeoisie, even when it claimed to transcend class barriers or laboured under the illusion that it pervaded all classes in the same way. Indeed it has been a truly bourgeois Church, if the notion of interclassism is taken as part of bourgeois ideology.[17]

An Interclass Reading of the Bible Is Possible

Even acknowledging the fact of oppression in society and the fact that there are oppressors and oppressed, the Christian does not give to that alignment the almost ontological character that Marxism gives to it. For the

53

gospel the line that divides men is a different one. We could simply say that Christ makes the difference: men in Christ and men apart from Christ; men under the lordship of Christ and men in rebellion against the One who should be their Lord. Regardless of their social standing, men that come under the lordship of Christ start a new lifestyle that in many cases could mean a total social realignment. In fact, we have to stress that biblical teaching gives a definite historical content to our obedience to Christ. Christ's lordship is no metaphysical premise, but a fact established in history by His resurrection. The lordship of Christ over human lives is also expressed in concrete actions of obedience that can be perceived in history. Because of that there is a way of being among the poor that follows the example, the intention, and the style of Jesus, and because of that it differs in intention, content, and style from the Marxist or any other way of being among the poor.

What missionary action needs today is to recover the awareness that God dwells with the poor and has a kind of preference for the poor, that there is a biblical teaching about justice to the poor and oppressed and that we have the example of Jesus Himself, of Paul and the primitive church, as well as that of the best missionary moments of the church about a way of being among the poor with the efficacy of *Agape* which is not necessarily the efficacy of a given political programme.[18] Missionary action also needs to remember from its biblical standard and its historical development that the repentance to which Jesus Christ calls us today may mean for some men the opening of their eyes to their condition as oppressors, and the change of their social practices.

The vision of the world divided between oppressors

and oppressed within a well-defined political context is linked to a global project and a vision of the future which today challenges any Christian reference to social justice. The vision of a revolution that puts an end to classes and oppression forces us into the consideration of another dilemma: reform or revolution. From the consideration of it we expect in the next chapter to complete our reflection on missions and social justice.

Notes

1. Dennis Goulet, "The World of Underdevelopment: A Crisis in Values," *The Christian Century* (April 24, 1974), p. 452.

2. Jose Miguez Bonino, "Christians and the Political Revolution," in *The Development Apocalypse*, a RISK paperback (Geneva: WCC, 1967), pp. 103-104.

3. John Gatu, "Missionary: Go Home," in *In Search of Mission*, IDOC, number 9 in the series *The Future of the Missionary Enterprise*, p. 70.

4. John V. Taylor, *CMS Newsletter*, No. 381 (May 1974), pp. 1-2.

5. Goodall, *op.cit.*, p. 23.

6. "Why the Condor," in *The Enterprise*, magazine of the Canadian Baptist Overseas Mission Board, Toronto (January 1974), pp. 5-6. See also Orville E. Daniel, *Moving with the Times* (Toronto: CBOMB, 1973), pp. 104-105.

7. Christian Lalive D'Epinay, *Haven of the Masses* (Surrey, England: Lutterworth-Friendship, 1969), pp. 143-144.

8. McGavran, *op.cit.*, p. 236.

9. *Ibid.*, p. 248.

10. From the almost 500 written responses that the author received on his paper "Evangelism and Man's Search for Justice, Freedom, and Fulfillment," in the Lausanne Congress on Evangelism, over a hundred quoted this verse as a proof of the uselessness of social concern.

11. A helpful treatment of the subject is Albert Gelin, *Les Pauvres de Yahve* (Paris: Ed. du Cerf, 1953).

12. See the last two chapters of Gelin.

3

REFORM, REVOLUTION, AND MISSIONS

Samuel Escobar

> The Lord looks out from heaven,
> he sees the whole race of men;
> he surveys from his dwelling-place
> all the inhabitants of earth.
> It is he who fashions the hearts of all men alike,
> who discerns all that they do. Psalm 33:13-15, NEB.

These words of the psalmist give us an insight into God's concern for all mankind. They belong to that biblical universal vision that the Jews were so prone to forget. Israel was constantly tempted to turn God into a national deity, their national deity. And the church is also tempted to think that God is only interested in what is going on inside the church. There is room in the heart of God for all people!

I like to read as a New Testament commentary on the verses of this psalm what Matthew says at the end of chapter 9. This Lord who "looks out from heaven" could be mistakenly seen as a detached deity who watches human tragedy as a nice show that entertains him, very much in the Greek fashion. But Matthew says:

> So Jesus went round all the towns and villages teaching in their synagogues, announcing the good news of the Kingdom, and curing every kind of ailment and disease. The sight of the people moved him to pity: they were like sheep without a shepherd, harassed and helpless. Matthew 9:35-37, NEB.

The eyes of the Lord of whom the psalmist speaks are also the eyes of the Lord of whom Matthew speaks. What He sees moves Him to compassion. But here we have Him in the midst of the crowd participating in the human condition. Such is the context of the call to mission: "*Then* He said to His disciples" and He called them to action. Presence, compassion, proclamation, and action. This is the universal concern out of which springs missionary action.

Ethical Dilemmas of Global Awareness

The global vision of which the psalmist speaks is part of the view of mankind's history as one universal reality that is being rediscovered painfully as we said in the previous chapter. This awareness has some embarrassing and difficult consequences when we come to the issue of poverty: the notion that poverty in one part of the world is linked to affluence in another. The Lausanne Covenant states:

58

All of us are shocked by the poverty of millions and disturbed by the injustices which cause it. Those of us who live in affluent circumstances accept our duty to develop a simple life-style in order to contribute more generously to both relief and evangelism.[1]

During the discussion of the text of the covenant the first sentence was very controversial for some, to the point that there were some pressures to have it eliminated, especially the last part: "the injustices which cause it." Theoretically at least it would not be difficult for anyone to accept that there is poverty and even to go as far as to accept that Christians should live a simple lifestyle. But it seems that Evangelicals are especially reluctant to accept the idea that poverty is caused by injustice, that the poverty of millions could be directly linked to the existence of a system that is basically unjust.

This global awareness with its consequent ethical challenges is key for understanding the acute question of a choice between Reform and Revolution.

Theological Dialogue on Political Issues

The path of theological dialogue on political and social issues is infested with traps of which we have to be constantly aware. A very apt warning is given to us by Alan Booth, who worked for several years in the Commission of International Affairs of the WCC. In a short but seminal book, *Christian Nonconformity in International Affairs*, he writes:

Laymen do not like the tendency of prelates to pronounce as though from some theological mountaintop, on questions they manifestly do not fully understand. Worse still, laymen are not normally given to "pronouncing" much at all. Their

59

daily lives are less conditioned by pulpit experience than by the effort to make an awkward sort of world work reasonably well for another year or two. The two styles of life make for very different preoccupations when it comes to thinking what is the best thing to be done next in international construction . . . perhaps as we press on into the bewildering future, one of the most dangerous failures of understanding will be between those who get "stuck in" to manipulating as best they can the system as they inherited it, learning the skills and devices which make it possible to stir it roughly in a tolerable direction and those so appalled by its potentialities that they withdraw into the rather unrewarding activity of being negative commentators. If that happens, we must see that neither group claims that it is "the church." Rather we must struggle on, trying to hold both within the one argumentative family. . . .[2]

There is a need for dialogue between those who are practitioners in the mission of the church in grass-roots situations around the world and those who are thinking and reflecting about the mission of the church in relation to social and political realities. We need to find the theological point of encounter where reflection comes to grips with issues that are real and not theoretical, issues that come from *down there* where missionary action is taking place. Just now, as we write, missionaries confront acute problems as their work relates to social and political issues. Whatever the pain of making those daily events the subject of reflection we have to face it.

From Daily Events to Global Analysis

In another chapter of this book John Driver quotes a letter from a missionary. From the same set of correspondence I want to quote a paragraph from another letter as a case that can start us in our understanding of the need for a global analysis. The letter was dated February 1971 and sent from Quito, Ecuador:

> Twenty-five years ago the Shell Oil Company lost many workers to Auca spears. For several reasons, Shell decided to leave Ecuador. Suddenly, with the discovery of a vast reserve of oil under the eastern jungle, 21 companies are working 1,500 men there. As they advance, we fly ahead of them and explain to Aucas living in their path that they are coming. We persuade them that they should move out of the way. This is done by Auca Christians through a loudspeaker mounted on the plane. As the Indians move, we notify the oil companies. As a result of this close coordination by radio and telephone through our Quito office, there has not been one life lost to date. *Praise God!*[3]

The immediate and forceful concern for the writer as well as for the readers, I hope, comes in that last line I have quoted: "there has not been one life lost to date." One way or other lives are saved. Though related only in style, these lines remind me of the twenty-seventh chapter of Acts where we have the story of Paul's sea trip to Rome and the storm he faced on the way. The apostle's faith, character, and leadership qualities are dramatically portrayed by Luke, as well as his realistic way of appraising situations and acting in them. At a given moment, the sailors want to leave the boat and Paul speaks to the military men in charge: "Unless these men stay on board you can none of you come off safely." Centurion and soldiers act immediately. After a final effort and when close to the end the soldiers want to kill the prisoners; the centurion saves their lives because he wants to save Paul's life. In the end "*all came safely to land.*"

Like our letter-writing missionary, like Luke, I myself

61

have as part of my biblical heritage the conviction that one life is important, that no single life is dispensable, not even the life of a prisoner or an Auca Indian. This great biblical truth was dramatically expressed by the Methodist writer Colin Morris in a BBC program: "I do not think the entire space programme is worth the life of a single hungry child."[4] Could this be an overstatement?

I want to believe that the strength of the missionary letters I have quoted is the concern for the lives of the Aucas. But this alone does not make us entirely happy with the letter. We read of oil that has been discovered, we see the name of Shell, a well-known oil company, and we start to realize the complications of the situation portrayed. Reflection takes me to an analysis that sooner or later missionary leaders and executives will have to make in relation to their missionary activities. Reflection comes at two levels. First: we saved some lives. That is the daily immediate situation. But then we go further and we ask other questions that aim to take a view of the whole missionary presence and the larger range of its action. What were the Aucas saved for? Who was interested in saving their lives? Why? Why was Shell Company linked to the mission and the missionary? What kind of relationship existed between them? In other words, we want to see the larger picture of missionary daily events and activities.

On the basis of a global analysis that takes into account these key questions and abundant information about the missionary practices of Roman Catholic and Protestant missions among the Latin American Indians, a group of social scientists has asked a complete halt to missionary activity: "As a result of this analysis we conclude that the suspension of all missionary activity is the most appropiate policy on behalf of Indian society as well as the moral integrity of the churches involved."[5] This sweeping statement is part of the now famous "Declaration of Barbados," around which there was an intense debate in mission circles. It could be easily dismissed as an outburst typical of the current tide against Western missionary activity. However there are now governments in Latin America that have adopted policies following that global analysis and the conclusions that it supported. And there are also ecclesiastical pressure groups advocating such policies in different parts of the world. Missions would do well to at least understand the situation.

Christian Global View from a Missionary Perspective

There is one kind of global view or analysis that is based on Christian presuppositions about the mission of the church, the proclamation of the gospel, and the meaning and end of history. Giving primacy to the extension of the church around the world as the central part of her mission, this view understands everything else, including human history and social processes as nothing but the setting inside which the real mission happens. We could say that basically this view is what seems to lie at the basis of the missionary letter from Ecuador that we quoted above. There is no value judgement about the goodness or the evil of Shell Oil's expansion into the jungles of Ecuador and the process of displacement of the Aucas to give way to "civilization." The whole process is probably seen as the necessary setting to let missionaries do their work. It does not belong to the essence of Christian mission to judge the process, to give an opinion about it, or to keep a certain distance from it for the sake of Christian identity.

63

There has not been enough reflection in missionary circles about the relationship between this tacit or explicit acceptance of contemporary Western economic and cultural expansion and the validity of a Christian mission so closely attached to it. In relation to past empires there are efforts, even in conservative circles, to clarify the issues. Take for instance this statement from Warren Webster:

> Some critics allege that Christianity is and always was the handmaiden of imperialism. This is a widely current falsehood which deserves to be labeled for what it is. In many places the mission of the Christian church has spread in spite of rather than because of Western diplomatic and commercial interests whose representatives have often impeded the spread of the Gospel, both through direct opposition and through personal lives that sometimes reflect the worst rather than the best of Christian culture.[6]

This was said in 1971, precisely the same year in which the letter from Ecuador we have quoted was written. However, the relationship between past imperialism and missionary work seems to be everywhere an embarrassing thing of the past and I have not found any statement favoring such alliance today. There seems to be a consensus, as we pointed out in our reference to McGavran in the previous chapter, that the postcolonial situation is better than the previous one, from the viewpoint of social justice and progress.

Ralph Winter has offered us an insightful description of the social and political processes that surrounded missionary work in the twenty-five years following the Second World War. Some of his statements are valuable for our consideration.

64

A factor tending to counterbalance the withdrawal of political imperialism was a heightened economic imperialism. The impingement of Western industrial and business enterprises upon the non-Western peoples generally increased . . . in some cases the withdrawal of the colonial governments gave a freer reign to Western business enterprises than was the case prior to independence. . . . The scope of economic imperialism was inevitably widened by the enormously increased industrial power of the Western heartland in Europe and America.[7]

What one does not find in Winter's book is a theological evaluation of the process he so aptly describes. Such evaluation could really mean a global analysis inside which it would be possible to understand missionary activity today, framing it in a way that would be faithful to biblical revelation. In the absence of such theological analysis we are left only with a pragmatism that moves into inconsistencies, posing serious ethical questions when it comes to the issue of social justice.

The fact that there is no clear theological analysis does not mean a complete absence of theological presuppositions with their consequent ethical preferences and decisions. The implicit presuppositions come to light at certain critical points that conservative evangelical missions face. The following excerpts from a prayer letter circulated by a mission working in South America is a good example.

Communism was reported to be making sweeping gains. Properties owned by foreigners were being seized by students. Extreme nationalism linked with strong anti-imperialism ran rampant on every side. Missionaries became suspect and their apprehension grew daily. Bolivian pastors and leaders in the churches feared that mission

65

properities would be seized by communists. We shared their concern. Things looked difficult for the missionaries and much prayer ascended that we might know His will. Then the miraculous took place. In three or four days of bloody revolution, the tide suddenly turned, the government was overthrown, communists were expelled from many places of leadership the rightists took control and hope brightened for the future. We knew anew that God is sovereign in all circumstances and that He was giving us further opportunity to win this nation to Christ.[8]

Absent from the text of this letter is any reference to reasons that would make one sociopolitical system more desirable than another for the Bolivian people. It seems that the basic concerns lay at the danger to "properties owned by foreigners," "suspicion about missionaries," and "mission properties seized by communists." When the situation was reversed we are told that "hope brightened for the future," but it is not clear for whose future. We can take the final line we have quoted as the expression of the main concern of the missionaries and we have to acknowledge their right to make that the aim in the light of which everything else has to be evaluated. Precisely what is missing in modern evangelical missiology is the articulation of such an aim in relation to the thorny issues of social justice, conflicts of interests between foreign-based agencies and national majorities, relationship between the aim "win a nation to Christ" and the biblical teaching about the kind of society for which Christians should work as part of their testimony. What missiologists need is to pursue the theological reflection that, from a different perspective, Max Warren started two decades ago.[9] This is a necessary task, especially in view of revolutionary global analysis.

66

Revolutionary Global Analysis

There is another kind of global analysis of the world situation and of the Christian mission which basically questions the whole Western capitalistic enterprise as we know it in the world today. It has been embraced by outspoken Christians in different parts of the world and applied to the understanding of Christianity itself, as the following paragraph shows:

> The ideological character ... of the manifestations of "sociological Christianity" can be unmasked only through the analysis of the functions it excercises within the modes of production and the socio-economic formations. Only in this way, analyzing the social systems' mechanisms of attraction and introjection, will it be possible to understand the frequent emasculation of the original liberating dynamic of Christianity.[10]

This methodology of "unmasking" the missionary enterprise by analyzing the functions it exercises in a given social and economic situation has been applied by movements like Christians for Socialism, and the Theology of Liberation.[11] From this perspective, for instance the process that we described in section 6 of the first chapter should be understood in a different way. Protestants in Latin America are seen as "ideological allies of foreign and national forces that keep the countries in dependence and the people in slavery and need ... contributing to create a benevolent and idealized image of the colonial powers (mainly the U.S.A.) which has disguised the deadly character of this domination."[12] We can understand better this analysis if we see the way it is applied to evaluate the missionary enterprise among native groups in different parts of the world.

For hundreds of years the collusion of government, religious and commercial interests has brought about the genocidal displacement and concentration of indigenous peoples living on the frontiers of capitalism. While "Christianizing savages" missionaries have seldom questioned the "need" for taking the lands of tribal people, but rather have seen it as the "inevitable advance of civilization." Believing themselves the harbingers of "modern civilization" they have in fact served as a cultural vanguard of a massive robbery on the frontiers of imperialist expansion, with no regard for the sovereign dignity of native peoples. Certain mission agencies, attempting to make aggression seem less cruel, have provided a velvet gloved alternative to the iron fist of armed conquest. As a pacification force they have used religion to substitute "peace" (surrender) and "hope" (promise of reward in an after life) for "death and destruction". . . . In the last hundred years however, so much gold, oil and uranium have been discovered on these otherwise unusable lands that "democratic governments" are becoming embarrassed to be seen repeatedly turning over the reservations to business interests. Thus, a new strategy has been adopted by many countries (such as Brazil and Colombia). Instead of treating indigenous peoples as conquered nations with rights, these are regarded as backward sectors of the conquering nation who have to be "educated and integrated" into it. The objective of these integration policies is to remove the tribal peoples in order to complete the control of national territory by the dominant class of the prevailing national group.[13]

The analysis takes us through two stages. First is the oppression from the prevailing national group against the small minorities which live in a tribal situation. The nation extends its frontiers without any regard for the rights of these peoples to live in their own land, in their own way. Such a process is taking place right now in several countries around the Amazonian basin. But there is a second level of relationships. Foreign national or multinational companies exert also an exploitative action to which governments bow because they are immersed in a situation of dependence for which the technical word of this analysis is imperialism.

When this analysis is pursued we find that its basic presupposition is the questioning of the whole Western capitalistic expansion process, the abolition of the system inside which the activities of companies like Shell Oil are possible. No other way is seen to put an end to exploitation and oppression. Local missionary action can thus be evaluated only in the light of the global picture, and thus is condemned. What is new in the way some Christians have accepted this analysis is the effort to relate it to the contents of Christian faith. The first paragraph we quoted in this section not only describes the role that "sociological Christianity" has played inside the system, but it also blames it for "emasculating the original liberating dynamic of Christianity." In other words, previous ways of doing missionary work have to be abandoned for a new way. Who is going to define it? How is it going to be defined? These are the key questions to be answered as this analysis is evaluated by the Christian. But again we have to ask the question posed before. What has been the exact relationship between Western capitalist expansion and missionary advance in our own century? To what degree does this relationship have to be evaluated and changed? How can it be understood in light of social trends in the world?

An important aspect of this analysis is that it cannot be taken apart from the global project to which it is linked. For the analysis to be truly revolutionary it must have an idea of the kind of system that would be implanted if the existing one is scrapped. What role is assigned to the church in the new system? Who assigns it? To what degree will that role be in accordance with the demands of the gospel and the whole of the biblical message? If criticism of the past way of accomplishing the Christian mission has to be taken seriously by the Christian, in view of the revolutionary analysis, the way the mission of the church is visualized inside the new system that revolutionaries aim to establish is also a matter of serious concern for the Christian today.

Reform or Revolution?

The new global awareness in the world has also brought an awareness of the colossal problems that mankind is facing. On the surface, some of them are evidently the result of human use of technological developments that could be described as neutral in themselves from the ethical viewpoint. As we have already said these problems not only are the context of missionary work today, but sometimes they are the result of missionary work. The missionary presence has sometimes been the prime mover of social change. Total indifference to the acute global problems that mankind faces today is not possible for the missionary minded Christian. Not even a pragmatic strategist of missions like McGavran can remain indifferent to them. From a Latin American perspective, borne out in a continent where the role of the masses is a matter of acute political debate, for instance, one cannot but pause to read these lines:

This is not only the age of the common man, but the future belongs to him. Mission policies should not be determined on the basis of the aristocratic order which dominated the world a few years ago. What God requires of His Church is based upon the forms that society is going to take, not those that flourished a hundred years ago. Christian mission stands at one of the turning points of history. A new order is being born. Its exact form is hidden from us; the forces which combine to make the new world are far too complex to allow anyone a clear view of the outcome. Yet it seems reasonably certain that, whatever else happens, the common man is going to have a great deal more to say in the future than he has in the past.[14]

In the same way, a conservative evangelical effort to deal seriously with the problem of hunger, to understand its global dimension and try to answer with a sense of urgency and a pragmatic stance, cannot but realize the need to deal with the systems in either a reformist or a revolutionary manner:

At the heart of the problems of poverty and hunger, injustice and inequity, are human systems which ignore, mistreat and exploit man made in the image of God. If humanity is to be served, if the hungry are to be fed, if the poor are to share in God's bestowed abundance, some of the systems will require drastic adjustments while others will have to be scrapped altogether.[15]

An illustrative European example of a Christian effort to deal with the dilemma is the document *The Church and the Powers* which was prepared by a work group in the French Protestant Federation.[16] In its moment it provoked a heated debate which may not have had the transcendance that it promised initially. The authors outline carefully the reformist and the revolutionary alternatives in the French context, but their consideration has a global reference. The reformist stance is presented as the

71

product of an *accord* that should follow awareness. This is the way it is described:

> Obviously this idea of accord is a very ambiguous one. Taken in an extremely broad sense it could denote the prospect of a radical transformation of the whole of economic activity and its political implications. The development of science and technology is in fact of interest to the institutions of government and administration and to all socio-economic groups involved with them and of concern to them. It can provide them with the means of combining in a joint strategy for the achievement of political objectives, if they are really serious about this. If certain conditions are met—in particular, the condition that action should not be narrowly confined to a national scale, but also the condition that curbs on freedom of enterprise should not be rejected out of hand—there is no technical reason why government guided by a more enlightened and better informed public opinion should not set itself the task of gradually eliminating social injustice, the task of protecting fundamental individual and political liberties, the task of reducing the brutality of the competitive system.[17]

The revolutionary stance is then outlined on the basis of the impossibility of radical reforms in captialism. A Marxist analysis of society and of recent history is applied to demonstrate the inherent tendency in capitalism "to impose the rule of the strongest":

> Capitalist society has not modified its structure in any radical way, even though it may have altered certain aspects of them or appeared to do so. Over against the mass of workers who are driven to sell their labour, certain groups, certain individuals, generally belonging to one social class, or accepted into this class because of their education and function, own or control the means of production, buy the labour they need, decide how the surplus value is to be used

by commandeering the profits, determine investment policy—all this because they have the power to decide and the authority.[18]

For the revolutionary analysis the state itself is unable to change things because it is not neutral:

> The State is not the sovereign impartial arbiter, the reconciler of the divergent interests of the various "social categories." It is commandeered today by castes allied by origin, culture, and interest; it is in the hands of the people with economic power. And these are often the same people who in succession—and sometimes simultaneously—are ministers, administrators, heads of the army and police, owners of the means of production and of the means of "communication."[19]

Though the document is evidently a juxtaposition of varied elements and it leaves open the choice for the Christians to whom it is addressed, the strength of the argument as presented in it goes to the revolutionary analysis. It criticizes acidly the relationship between the churches and the established order in France and it presents as entirely new the ethical challenges of the new situation, which demand a Christian participation in the change of collective structures. The existing system and its ideology are considered intolerable in such a way that

> those who desire to live in the hope opened up to us by the Gospel (are prompted) to reject the *status quo* root and branch and to adopt one or other of the options mentioned above, namely, either a critical approach aiming at a bold reformism or a revolutionary attitude of opposition and challenge.[20]

In Latin America, as in other parts of the Third World, Marxism has taken the initiative in the realm of ideology, infiltrating almost every revolutionary movement. Its claim to be "scientific" gives it an exclusivist tendency. We have to take that into account because the term "reformist" has become very misleading in the political debate. Reformist is not synonymous with "conservative" or "opposed to real change," as Marxists and their followers suggest. The lack of a well-defined, coherent, and easy to communicate ideology in the West, especially when it comes to understanding issues like history or social justice, does not make Marxism automatically true, or "scientific." The most serious criticism of some forms of theology of liberation comes precisely at this point. Borrowing a language and a methodology has meant also borrowing an exclusivist way of understanding history, the biblical message, and the available political options.

The three examples we have quoted in this section are efforts to try to understand the mission of the church or one aspect of it inside a global view of our world and our history at this point. The first two are just hinting at the problem; the third has gone further but has probably oversimplified the alternatives. However, missionary statesmen cannot go on avoiding the issue forever.

A Christian Criticism of the System

We have to ask the question about the possibility of developing a critical approach and a global vision on biblical and historical grounds that are specifically Christian and do not rest basically on a given political and sociological analysis. Is there something like a gospel-based critical stance?

This is the point at which I think that the Anabaptist position can bring an element of renewal to theology and church life in the West. Long before a global analysis of capitalism was developed along historical and structural lines, there was a questioning of every system on theological grounds. There was, moreover, a way of life that could be lived under very different circumstances. It could be briefly described as a consistent refusal to accept wholeheartedly any existing system or to give a Christian official sanction to it. It involves a view of the uniqueness of the people of God and the unique nature of their mission, and a view of the origins, dynamism, and end of history. It means to begin with, in the words of Walter Klaassen, an understanding of the nature of the Christian life as discipleship and a view of the church as the company of those consciously committed to Jesus.

A church that understands herself along these lines can face any kind of situation with a missionary mind and vocation. When we take into account the proposals that have been discussed in the last decades in relation to restructuring the missionary enterprise we realize that the boldest changes would demand this kind of vision. Moreover, when we see the type of church that has been able to survive when the advantages of Constantinianism were taken from Christians, we find the same type of self-understanding and missionary presence.

A careful consideration of a gospel-based understanding of our global situation could help us also not to repeat the past mistakes of answering to the demands of a new situation with the resources of the spirit of our age rather than with the resources of God's Word. Wilbert Shenk has outlined the way in which the different stages in missionary development have followed Western expansion in concept and method. He concludes that "we are always creatures of the times in which we live but we

75

ought to exercise much critical evaluation rather than bowing to what seems to be inevitable."[21]

Marxism is the official religion in one part of the world. Old ethnic religions are becoming the ideology of new or renewed nationalisms. Christian mission cannot be accomplished if Western Christians make the gospel the official ideology of the West, because in order to do so they will have to change it, taking from it precisely the elements that would be the basis of a biblical critical stance, in the same fashion in which it would have to be changed if it were to become a "useful instrument for revolution" and perhaps the official religion of the future post-revolutionary society.

Consequences for Mission

From the perspective of Christian mission the issues we have examined are urgent ones. Transnational missionary work is done inside the framework of international relations which can change radically as countries follow reform, revolution, or realignments. Frequently, from the viewpoint of the revolutionary, the foreign missionary whose presence is possible because of a system of relationships is lending justification to the existing order, by his very presence. Moreover, if the message of the missionary has elements that foster a passive acceptance of the existing order, or a total refusal to deal with it critically, his presence is interpreted as active cooperation with the perpetuation of the system. This is even more true, of course, if missionary activity lends itself obviously to the service of business interests or the national interests of the missionary's country.[22]

(1) If I go back to the biblical model of missionary advance that I consider normative for our own situation, I

76

find elements that can help to understand anew these issues. The world of Paul the missionary and the primitive church was the world of the *Pax Romana.* Its presence permeates the pages of the New Testament. We find it carefully depicted as the background of missionary advance that conditioned such advance but also registered its impact. What I do not find in the pages of the New Testament is a cult of the *Pax Romana,* made up of enthusiasm or wholehearted identification with it. It is true that we could say that appealing to Roman citizenship, as Paul did, could sometimes bring the advantages of not being flogged, or of a fair judicial treatment not available to everyone else[23]—advantages similar to those that carrying an American, Canadian, or Swiss passport could mean today. But there is no blessing or consecration of the Roman Empire nor is the church put at the service of its agencies. We must grasp the basis and the working out of this combination of acceptance and detachment, especially in light of later developments like the Book of Revelation. In its ethos and basic stance the modern missionary enterprise needs to develop a truly biblical attitude toward the *Pax Americana.* This is especially necessary for evangelicals whose role in the U.S.A. has been changing.[24]

(2) The question of the structures and practices of the missionary enterprise has to be dealt with in a similar fashion. How many missionary policies are nothing but the reflection of the commercial and imperial practices of the *Pax Americana?* This is not a weakness peculiar of Anglo-Saxon character but of imperial practices. I have already witnessed the difficulties of Brazilian missionaries in Bolivia and of urbanite Argentinians among the Indians in the rural north of their country, enough to

realize that it is the system of their society which shapes their practices. It is the uncritical acceptance of a system of thought and practice (a way of organizing people, basic notions about property, relationships, initiative, etc., all of them borrowed from the society around), which has entered into missionary policies that need drastic revision.

The uniqueness of missionary structures and practices as we find them in Scripture has to rediscovered. These structures reflect a concept of man before God, man in Christ, and man in community. A key characteristic of Anabaptist theology is the conviction that the presence of the people of God, by its ethos, structure, and practices *is already* the presence of the new, the presence of the kingdom. This kind of emphasis is needed as a balance to another way of visualizing the future of mission, exemplified by Winter in the following paragraphs:

> More than ever, the shape of tomorrow will be the result of the conscious design and remodeling of structures rather than gradual unintentional development. A century of amateurish and merely intuitive groping characterized the Age of Revolution in the Marxian period in regard to the conscious modification of the structures of society. But in the new period, first in business and industrial circles, and then finally in civil and ecclesiastical spheres, a much matured systems engineering, sophisticated by additional insights from anthropology, sociology and social psychology, will enable a much more effective reevaluation of church structures, denominational and local.[25]

The wisdom of this age, yes, provided it does not contradict the basic requirement of revealed wisdom as to the nature and shape of the mission. The correction comes immediately as we see a case in point. After the statement we have quoted, Winter goes on to give examples of restructuring. The much debated issue of foreign agencies parallel to national churches is considered and here is the conclusion:

> Perhaps through structural remodeling a new kind of agency can be established which will retain the mobility and initiative of the paternalistic mission, yet neither be supervisory nor competitive to the younger church, nor even necessarily structurally related to it.[26]

Good intentions indeed! But it all depends. Structural relation may be the only way to avoid competitiveness between two partners with very different financial power. As Wilbert Shenk has pointed out, there is a contrast between the power and influence of a mission, made possible and protected through bureaucracy, and the relatively weak position of a new church made up of economically disadvantaged members.[27] It is evident that restructuring demands a return to scriptural principles that may be in open contrast with the "free market competition" principle of the *Pax Americana*.

(3) A critical stance toward the system in which we live should not be a paralyzing exercise in relation to the demands of God's mission for His people today. The fact that Christians uncover the guilt of the West should not paralyze Western Christians into inaction and passivity. Whatever the critical nature of the task of becoming aware of global realities it should not make Western churches less mission minded. Asked about America's responsibility to the world situation in view of temptations to imperialism and intervention, John Howard Yoder stressed the need for a renewed sense of mission. "I do not think the alternative is to stay home and just

pile it up more."[28] And then he went on outlining possibilities which ranged from the internationalization of help to the resignation of American citizenship—all of them feasible for anyone who takes seriously the mission of God and is ready to pay the cost about which so many songs speak eloquently.

It is evident that another practice that goes against the basic presuppostions of the *Pax Americana* is that you can serve and invest without expecting personal or institutional gain. You can serve and invest where the needs are greater and you can educate your churches at home to overcome their capitalist mentality in that area. Whatever provision we make in our concepts for the urgency of evangelization, it is evident that the mission of the people of God does not stop at that point. Younger dynamic churches today need ministries from their sister churches which are rendered as service that does not expect compensation—not even the compensation of the growth of the particular brand of Christianity to which we belong. "Foreign help" has become a euphemism that covers a multitude of sins in international relationships today. It is the imperial practice of the capitalist as well as the socialist nations. It is a fact that charity is no substitute for justice and that justice sometimes makes charity unnecessary. The time has come for the Christian community to apply the justice of the kingdom inside her universal dimensions.

(4) Biblical eschatology must shape missions, biblically understood. The global revolutionary analysis applied to the understanding of the history of Christian missions evaluates this according to revolutionary aims and goals. When shaped by Marxism, revolutionary analysis becomes based on Marxist eschatology. From that view-

point the failure or success of the missionary task of the
church is measured by her failure or success in promoting
the cause of Marxist revolution, i.e., providing the steps
toward a classless society.

The biblical basis of missions must be restated at this
point. As Douglas Webster has said:

> Jesus achieved what he was sent to do because he was not
> concerned with the categories of success and failure as
> understood by the world. Because he was content to appear
> to fail in the sight of men, if this had to be the cost of wit-
> ness to the truth and obedience to God, his mission gained
> an effectiveness which became universal. There is reason to
> suppose that the pattern of the Church's mission, at least in
> some countries, may not be altogether dissimilar. It could at
> one and the same time seem to be a total failure in the eyes
> of men and yet, by its faithfulness in obedience and witness,
> be the means of achieving God's will ultimately in those
> countries.[29]

Falling into the theological trap of identifying the
Marxist classless society with the kingdom of God, and
the steps of the Marxist strategy with the "signs" of the
kingdom of God, will only limit our perception of the
mission of the church, the history of that mission in our
world, and the ways of accomplishing it today.

But there is a second reflection necessary here. What
we understand by social justice has to be shaped by our
biblical stance. From that perspective Marxist achievements have to be evaluated, and from that perspective
also Christian achievements throughout history have to
be evaluated. It can only distort theological discourse
and missionary practice if Marxist theory is used to
evaluate Christian empirical reality without any
reference to real social justice in those places where

81

Marxism has been applied and is being applied. In the same way, an important part of the missiology of the coming decades will be to pay attention to the way in which the church has accomplished her mission in countries where the Marxist utopia has shaped social change. In good Anabaptist fashion that observation will not only take into account the streams of Christianity that have an official blessing or have openly identified themselves with their system, but also those other streams of Christian faith and life which have kept the combination of acceptance and detachment to which we have referred above.

(5) A rediscovery of the radical uniqueness of the gospel is taking place around theological reflection on the mission of the church today. For too long there has been a truncated gospel announced in such a way that, as Stott has said, we have had "sermonettes that have breathed Christianettes." In the totality of the biblical message there is an element of rejection of idolatry. That includes the idolatry of the system. True mission involves living under the lordship of Christ and preaching against idols. No missionary is a true missionary if he does not live and announce the gospel in a way that makes clear that he does not worship Mammon or Caesar. This may make the missionary attractive for some revolutionaries and suspicious for others, attractive for some systems and suspicious for others. As we see in the New Testament itself, one and the same society may change its attitudes to the Christian presence according to its own historical dynamic. Mission stems from the uniqueness of the gospel, of Jesus Christ's mission and victory. Missions today have to be faithful to the gospel. They may be scandal and offense to many in the right and in the left.

But we have to be sure that the scandal is the scandal of the cross and not the scandal of the *Pax Americana* or of Western imperial advance.

Some of the most complicated social processes have swept the world in the first three fourths of our century: colonial expansion and decay, totalitarianism of the right and the left, massive movements of liberation that have changed the face of continents. However, we have enough information now to see even dimly that God's mission is being accomplished in amazing ways, against any kind of expectations and fears, in the midst of turmoil. The *Pax Brittanica* passed away. The *Pax Americana* and the *Pax Sovietica* show signs of fatigue, change, and even decay. Missionaries of Jesus Christ are challenged to live anew the justice of the kingdom, and to proclaim the just King.

Notes

1. *Lausanne Covenant*, paragraph 9.

2. Alan Booth, *Christian Nonconformity in International Affairs* (London: Epworth Press, 1970), pp. 10-11.

3. *IDOC-North America*, Number 51, "The Missionary and Social Justice: Latin America," II, Options and Strategies, p. 27.

4. Colin Morris, *What the Papers Didn't Say* (London: Epworth Press, 1971), p. 26.

5. "Declaration of Barbados," in W. Dostal, ed., *The Situation of the Indian in South America* (Geneva: WCC, 1972), p. 378. This volume includes several regional and national studies that were used in the symposium that produced the declaration. The July 1973 issue of the *International Review of Mission* was dedicated to a discussion of the Declaration and its aftermath.

6. Warren Webster, "Missions in Time and Space," in C. Peter Wagner, ed., *Church-Mission Tensions Today* (Chicago: Moody Press, 1972), p. 96.

7. Ralph D. Winter, *The Twenty-Five Unbelievable Years, 1945-1969* (Pasadena: William Carey Library, 1970), p. 14.

8. *IDOC-North America, op. cit.*, p. 28.

9. Max A. C. Warren, *Caesar the Beloved Enemy* (London: SCM Press, 1955). See especially the first chapter, "Some Notes for a Theology of Imperialism."

10. From the working document of the First Latin American Conference of Christians for Socialism (December 1971). Quoted in *NACLA's Latin America and Empire Report* (December 1973), p. 2.

11. Relationship between these two movements is described and explained in Jose Miguez Bonino, *Doing Theology in a Revolutionary Situation* (Philadelphia: Fortress Press, 1975). See especially "Introduction" and chapters I to IV.

12. *Ibid.*, pp. 17-18.

13. NACLA, *op.cit.*, p. 15.

14. McGavran, *op.cit.*, p. 259.

15. W. Stanley Mooneyham, *What Do You Say to a Hungry World?* (Waco: Word Books, 1975), p. 117. See also chapter 6.

16. English version published in *Study Encounter*, No. 3, 1972. For an assortment of French reactions see *Foi et Vie*, March-June, 1972, and *Icthus*, April-May, 1972. In both cases the whole issue of the magazine is dedicated to the document, *The Church and the Powers*.

17. *The Church and the Powers*, 5.2.

18. *Ibid.*, 6.2.1.

19. *Ibid.*, 6.2.5.

20. *Ibid.*, 7.1.2.

21. Wilbert R. Shenk, "Missions in Retrospect and Prospect," *Christianity Today* (July 28, 1972), p. 9.

22. At this point in history readers may be familiar with the alleged use of missionaries by agencies such as the American CIA. For one type of evangelical reaction see *Sojourners*, January 1976, and March 1976. For another type see *Christianity Today*, October 10, 1975, pp. 62-64.

23. A recent article about this issue is Boyd Reese, "The Apostle Paul's Exercise of His Rights as a Roman Citizen as Recorded in the Book of Acts," in *The Evangelical Quarterly* (July-Sept., 1975), pp. 138-145.

24. A candid description of the way in which the National Association of Evangelicals has come closer to Washington and the American government in the last decades can be seen in Clyde W. Taylor, "Remembering . . . We Press Forward," *Action* (Winter, 1974), pp. 14 ff.

25. Ralph Winter, *op.cit.*, p. 77.

26. *Ibid.*, pp. 77-78.

27. Wilbert R. Shenk, *op.cit.*, p. 9.

28. "Radical Christianity: An Interview with John Yoder," *Right On* (February 1975).

29. Douglas Webster, *Yes to Mission* (London: SCM, 1966), p. 35.

4

The Anabaptist Vision and Social Justice
John Driver

This study represents an attempt to understand the church's attitude toward, and role in, the contemporary struggle for social justice in Latin America from the perspective of classic Anabaptism and its vision of the church. It is not so much a historical study focusing on sixteenth-century Anabaptism as it is an attempt to understand the current struggle from that perspective. The fact that we are also Mennonites who share missionary concerns for Latin America leads us to take note of these two elements as well.

Anabaptism and the Struggle for Social Justice

A concern for social justice was probably more central to the genius of the Anabaptist movement of the sixteenth century than most modern Mennonites would imagine. While sixteenth-century Anabaptism was certainly a religious movement, it was also a social movement.

It is generally recognized that Anabaptism was one of a whole series of socioreligious movements throughout Europe during the Middle Ages which focused their social protest in terms of a call to "apostolic simplicity" in life and worship. This mood was shared by such diverse movements as medieval monasticism, the Waldensians, the renewal movement among the Franciscans and Joaquin de Fiore in Italy, the English Lollards, Peter Chelchitsky and the Bohemian Brethren, and Anabaptism. In these movements the concern for a return to "apostolic simplicity" responded in one way or another to social and economic dissatisfaction. While the Bible seemed to put a premium on poverty, the church came to own one third of the real estate of Europe and the income from it. The New Testament spoke of brotherhood, but this was contradicted by the church which legitimized class differences. These socioeconomic contradictions produced tensions which led to revolution.

Human misery was no doubt a prime cause of social dissatisfaction which led many to question the papacy, the hierarchy, and the church's social practices as well as its doctrines. One of the concrete expressions of this general mood of dissatisfaction was the series of peasant uprisings which took place in Europe in the late fifteenth and early sixteenth centuries, culminating in the Peasant Revolt of 1524-25. Recent studies have shown that the religious and social views held by the peasants and the Anabaptists overlapped considerably.[1] For our purposes a brief review of common social concerns must suffice.

87

(1) Both groups insisted that the gospel is relevant to social and economic realities.

(2) Both protested against the payment of tithes (since this merely increased the wealth of the church) as well as against the charging of interest (since this oppressed the poor and was also forbidden in Scripture). The peasants were willing to continue their payments if they were used to support local pastors and as relief for the poor.

(3) Both rejected structures which perpetuated class distinctions. This led to the rejection of the use of titles among Anabaptists and to the creation of brotherhood structures for the congregation. Among the peasants it meant that common woodlots, pastures, and waters should no longer be sequestered by the feudal lords for their exclusive use, but be available to all who needed them.

(4) Both called for human freedom. For the peasants this meant freedom from serfdom. For the Anabaptists it meant freedom to act and to believe according to one's own conscience without coercion.

(5) Both sought independence from ecclesiastical control. The peasants asked freedom to choose (and dismiss) their own pastors and to hear the pure preaching of the Word of God. Anabaptists not only demanded the same things, but set about to realize them in their clandestine conventicles.

(6) Both were movements of resistance to the established authorities (church and state). Peasants resisted the increasing economic demands of their feudal masters. Anabaptists resisted the claim of church hierarchies (both Catholic and Protestant) on their unquestioning obedience as well as rejecting the sacral claims of secular authorities.

(7) Both groups wanted nonviolent change to fuller social justice and equality. But the peasants were prepared to use force if necessary. As for the Anabaptists, there was some ambivalence among them prior to Schleitheim, noted especially in Hubmaier, Hut, and Anabaptists in the Tyrol. However, under the pressures of official persecution and through study of the Scriptures the doctrine of the two kingdoms established itself among Anabaptists. It became clear to them that there are two realms and that different sets of rules are operative in these two spheres: violence in one and nonresistance in the other.

It is possible that many of those who originally participated in peasant movements found their way into Anabaptist conventicles after their uprisings were crushed by authorities. The remarkable growth of Anabaptism in areas in which peasant revolts had been forcibly repressed points to this possibility. The brotherhood communities which characterized Anabaptists of all types, the more formally structured communities of the Hutterites as well as the less structured congregations of the Swiss and Dutch, gave concrete expression to the fundamental social concerns of the movement and assured its survival in the face of official persecution.

Concern for Social Justice in Latin America

The struggle for social justice in Latin America is as old as imperial domination itself. This fact is illustrated by a sermon preached in a straw-thatched church in Santo Domingo in the year 1511 by a Dominican friar, Antonio de Montesinos. Preaching from the text, "A voice cries in the wilderness . . ." Montesinos delivered the first deliberate and important public protest against social injustices in the New World. The following are excerpts from the sermon:

> In order to make your sins against the Indians known to you . . . I am a voice of Christ crying in the wilderness of this island. . . . This is going to be the strangest voice that ever you heard, the harshest and hardest and most awful and most dangerous that ever you expected to hear. . . . This voice says that you are in mortal sin, that you live and die in it, for the cruelty and tyranny you use in dealing with these innocent people. Tell me, by what right or justice do you keep these Indians in such a cruel and horrible servitude? . . . Why do you keep them so oppressed and weary, not giving them enough to eat nor taking care of them in their illness? For with the excessive work you demand of them they fall ill and die, or rather you kill them with your desire to extract and acquire gold every day. . . . Be certain that, in such a state as this, you can no more be saved than the Moors and Turks.[2]

Within three months orders issued in Spain called for the cessation of such scandalous protests. But voices raised in behalf of the Indians would not be silenced. The loudest of these was, without doubt, that of Bartolome de las Casas. Las Casas was originally a colonist who worked his mines and cultivated his estate with Indian slaves. "Converted" at the age of forty into a defender of the Indians, he dedicated the rest of his life (more than 50 years) to the struggle for justice. Las Casas insisted to his dying day that the Spanish conquest of the Americas was being waged by unjust means. He held that the only way to commend the gospel to the heathen is through peaceful means.

It is not surprising that today, almost five centuries later, Las Casas' writings still strike a sympathetic chord in Latin America. The very same injustices denounced by Montesinos are those which, in our times, have given rise to the so-called "theology of liberation." In the present "situation of sin" the exploitation may be less direct and the oppressors may be farther removed from the suffering, but it is no less real. The brief account of liberation theology which follows does not pretend to describe it as a system of theological reflection. Our purpose here is simply to point up its fundamental concern for social justice.

Theology of liberation is basically "reflection based on the Gospel and the experiences of men and women committed to the process of liberation in the oppressed and exploited land of Latin America . . . of shared efforts to abolish the current unjust situation and to build a different society, freer and more human."[3] This means that theological reflection is preceded by analysis of sociopolitical reality. The principal tool for this analysis is a "structuralistic" methodology which questions radically the prevailing social system in Latin America: one of economic, social, political, and cultural dependence from which people must be liberated as a necessary condition for their well-being. This is a system of theological reflection rooted in the oppression and exploitation of the Third World over against those theologies which are the products of the affluent world.

Rejecting both the oppression of foreign colonial powers (USA and Europe) and oligarchic minorities within Third World countries, as well as religious paternalism, everything connected with colonialism or neo-colonialism comes under judgment. Some churches have gone so far as to condemn the capitalistic system. The Latin American Catholic Council of Bishops implied

91

this in its Conference in Medellin (1968) and the Argentine Methodist Conference did so expressly in 1971. The consequence of this position is clear: it becomes a Christian duty to struggle against the present system and for the construction of a new one. In Latin America today this means concretely a decision for socialism, for revolution (however the form may be qualified), and for cooperation with left-wing political parties and movements.

Liberation Theology understands salvation in terms of socioeconomic liberation and the historic experience of the Exodus in the life of the people of God becomes the paradigm for the political liberation of men in all times.

Christ is understood preeminently in historical categories. The Word made flesh means, practically, that Christ is to be found in every man. Since God is found among men, we meet Him in "our encounter with men; we encounter Him in the commitment to the historical process of mankind."[4]

The church is to be a place of liberation in her concrete existence. But her character is provisional since she is oriented toward the reality of the kingdom of God, present in history in God's liberating action among men. The church is understood dynamically, rather than spatially. She is basically a calling—a vocation. All of mankind is understood as the people of God and, therefore, all of human history must be understood as a general history of salvation. The church is called to fulfill a service function within this history.

The experience of conversion is understood in political terms. To evangelize is to point out all situations of injustice and exploitation because they are incompatible with the gospel. This is made meaningful only by living and announcing the gospel from within a commitment to liberation, in solidarity with those who are exploited.

One is impressed by the way in which the so-called "Theology of Liberation" takes very seriously the struggle for social justice. In fact man's injustices toward his fellowman constitute its point of departure. Its insistence on taking seriously the concrete sociopolitical situation in which Christians find themselves is perhaps its greatest strength. However, the possible consequences of a hermeneutic in which the historical situation is normative probably represents its greatest danger.[5]

Contemporary Strategies Adopted by Christians Concerned for Social Justice in Latin America

(1) The first of these might be called the option of justifiable recourse to violence in the struggle for justice. As we have just noted, the movement which roughly corresponds to "Theology of Liberation" understands that the prevalence of socioeconomic injustices in Latin America is the basic problem around which the church should orient itself. "To struggle to establish justice among men is to begin to be just before the Lord; love of God and love of neighbour are inseparable."[6] Violence is not necessarily implicit in this struggle for justice but "when a government adopts repressive policies . . . uses violence and even torture on the men who are fighting for the liberation of their peoples, we propose that the church condemn such repressive methods, that it recognize the right these men possess to fight for justice, and that it manifest solidarity with their ideals, even though it may not always approve of their methods."[7] Some Christians, thrust into extreme situations, see no other way but the traditional one of fighting, opposing institu-

tionalized violence with counter-violence.

In reality, this position represents a type of theocratic option. In situations where change cannot be brought about without force, revolutionary violence is justified as a last resort. While traditional moralists have spelled out the necessary conditions for waging a just war, Third World theorists have been working on the criteria for determining when revolutionary violence is justifiable: (1) "if oppressors have already utilized violence," (2) "if all the possibilities for legal action and protest have already been exhausted without success," (3) "if the existing situation causes more human suffering than will probably result from revolutionary counter-violence."

Christian revolutionaires who opt for this strategy are generally persons of high moral sensitivity who are moved out of compassion for, and a feeling of solidarity with, masses who suffer under the effects of institutionalized violence of unjust systems.

(2) Another strategy is the "guerrilla option." Although it has considerable in common with the first strategy (its basic sociological analysis, its commitment to liberation, its understanding of the gospel and its implications, etc.), there is at least one fundamental difference. In the doctrine of the just revolution, as in the concept of the just war, violence is not justified unless there is reasonable assurance of success in the venture. Decisions are made on the basis of pragmatic calculations. However, some guerrilla movements consider the option of violence in terms not unlike those proper of the crusade (holy war). The "cause" is invested with a holy aura which is above ethical or pragmatic scrutiny. It is assigned a quasi-religious, absolute value to which the Christian may give himself fully. In fact there is the

possibility of martyrdom. The practical distinction between the just war (or just revolution) and the crusade (or guerrilla) is the latter's disposition to martyrdom. The first requires that justice be accomplished, even at the cost of violence. The second conceives of death as a morally valid sacrifice, not because ends have been realized, but in the glorious nature of death itself.

The following excerpts from a letter written by a South American Christian "guerrillero" illustrates the "guerrilla option":

> On joining the guerrillas . . . I believe that my true priestly consecration is beginning now—a consecration which demands total sacrifice so that all men might live, and live abundantly. . . . (Camilo) Torres' word and example are the banner of redemption . . . and a light on the path of all those who seek total commitment with the revolution. Camilo has not died; he lives in the hearts of the poor and oppressed, within each man who fights for justice and human brotherhood. . . . He was a prophet of our time, a total revolutionary, a new man of that future society which is in gestation. . . . It is to his attitude and thought that I owe the joy of the commitment which I announce, the decision to give myself, to death if necessary, for the liberation of the Colombian people. . . . The masses experience hunger, injustice, and exploitation. They need live examples to direct their rebelliousness and channel their eagerness for liberation. Camilo has done it. With his glorious sacrifice, he showed once for all the way of redemption for all revolutionaries and oppressed masses . . . from these mountains washed with the blood of our martyrs, I invite all Colombian men and women to organize and prepare for the final struggle, following the banner and example of the great teacher of our people, Camilo Torres Restrepo. With the strength that his glorious death imparts to us, together with my comrades I repeat: Not one step backwards—Liberation or death.[8]

(3) A third option is the nonviolent struggle for justice. The International Reconciliation Movement is representative of this position. Nonviolence is seen as a strategy for the liberation of man and the attainment of justice in his social relationships. This option is no less critical of the realities in Latin America than those already listed: oppression, both internal and external; unjust economic system which favors a few and leaves the majority condemned to a marginal existence; education which prepares people to serve the existing system; and so on.

In the struggle for justice this option attempts to practice the concepts lived and taught by Christ in His gospel of liberation. It believes that by His incarnation—attacking evil at its root in the conscience of man—by the power of truth, by the love and justice of God, and accepting all the consequences of these in his commitment until death, all the while fully respecting the human person, Christ brought the revelation of true liberation to all men. This process of liberation and reconciliation begins in the community of faith. "Christ . . . inspired the conversion of men so that they may be the leaven of the renewal of the world. Concretely, liberative action must be the ability to save ourselves, to transform ourselves in serving our neighbor. By themselves, . . . structures do not liberate . . . Christ proved his messianism by concrete and liberating actions. In the same way, the church must continue the liberating action of Christ among the brethren, the men who in Latin America suffer at present from oppression and dependence."[9]

Nonviolence which does not take a stand regarding the process of liberation of the people will be suspect. The

96

church is called to take this stand in the hope that oppressed peoples will actively participate in their liberation, assume personal and collective responsibility, and thereby make possible the liberation of their oppressors and the transformation of structures as well.

Since nonviolence is understood as a strategy for social change, Christians who take this option will be social activists, engaging in conscientization at all levels, in public manifestations, strikes, civil disobedience, etc., convinced that nonviolence will finally prevail over violence. Underlying this strategy is belief in the ultimate efficacy of nonviolence.

(4) Another option which is taken principally by Protestants is a sort of sociopolitical collaboration with the power structures in what is believed to be the long term interests of the church. Some Protestant missionaries in Chile, for example, welcomed the overthrow of Allende's government by the military junta because this assured them of "freedom" to evangelize and plant churches. In Bolivia a bloody revolution lasting three or four days and engineered by rightest military elements which toppled the government and expelled leftists from places of leadership was heralded by some as a miraculous event. "Hope brightened for the future. We knew anew that God is sovereign in all circumstances and that He was giving us further opportunity to win this nation to Christ. How thrilling to experience firsthand that our 'God only doeth wondrous things'—everything He does is miraculous."[10]

In January 1973, an interdemoninational group of Christians in Bolivia released a public statement calling for the cessation of a rising "spiral of violence" in that country. In his reply, the Minister of Interior, a colonel in

97

the Bolivian army, suggested that the foreigners in the group might do well to leave the country and then cited, with approval, the ministry of a charismatic Catholic healer and evangelist who preaches "peace, love, and the gospel." The implication in this instance was, of course, that to protest violence and call for its cessation is more of a threat to the power structures than preaching and healing.

This option assumes the position that if churches are simply left alone to evangelize and grow, the immediate problems of social justice in society can be overlooked in the hope that in the long run the church will be able to penetrate the social structures with its healing influence.

There is a sense in which the Church Growth Movement shares something of this general attitude, since it tends to relegate concerns for social justice to a position separate from, and posterior to, church planting concerns.

(5) An option acceptable to conservative Catholics, as well as Protestants, in Latin America is one which concerns itself with the conservation and strengthening of Christian social values. One small but militant group which is representative of this reactionary wing is a quasi-military Catholic movement dedicated to the conservation of "Tradición, Familia y Propiedad."

But many traditional Catholics and a considerable number of Protestants in Latin America would fall into this conservative category. The socioeconomic orientation of this group tends toward captialism rather than socialism; development rather than radical change of system; toward evolution rather than revolution. This orientation generally rejects socialization out of principle. It tends to see society (Latin American vestiges of

98

Christendom, in the case of Catholics, and Liberal
Democracy, in the case of Protestants) as fundamentally
Christian and basically sound. Therefore it proposes
progressive and gradual changes without endangering
the system. Social concern tends to be individualistic.
The rehabilitation of persons in need contributes to the
welfare of society. The exercise of repressive power, and
even of violence, is generally accepted as necessary since
it assures the maintenance of order in which this
progressive Christianization of social structures can take
place. This, of course, represents a fundamentally
Constantinian stance.

The Social Justice Strategies of Mennonites in Lower South America

It could probably be said, in a general way, that the
broad spectrum of social justice options which characterize the church at large in Latin America also
describe the situation of the Mennonite churches in
Lower South America.

(1) The theocratic vision of society and social justice is
manifest in the conviction that the church should be
God's instrument to extend His rule into the structures of
society with a view to transforming the civil community
into the community in which God's just social order is
recognized. In Latin America the proponents of this vision have generally realized that some recourse to violence may be necessary in order to achieve their ends.
Some go even farther, investing the social justice cause
with a sense of holy fervor similar to that which
characterized religious crusades in the past. These are
the "guerrillas."

A few Latin Mennonites in Uruguay and Argentina,

99

largely influenced by such movements as ISAL and Third World Catholic groups, have been sympathetic and even active in promoting this vision. However, I think that I am correct in saying that in no case has this theocentric vision of social transformation been really fanned into crusading ("guerrilla") fervor, although, in some cases, this has surely been a very real temptation.

(2) A spiritualizing approach to concern for social justice probably represents the most characteristic stance assumed by Mennonites in Lower South America. There is a basic concern for the conversion of the individual, first and foremost, because he will therefore be a better person. The concern for personal salvation does not seem to arise principally out of a concern for the kind of just social relationships which will necessarily characterize the people who are called by God's name. Of course, it is recognized that if enough people change their personal attitudes toward ethical questions such as money, race, power, etc., social structures might eventually change, but this is not their point of departure. Some, I suspect, are tempted to combine the spiritualistic and theocratic visions: hoping that the conversion of people in places of political power might lead to the establishment of a more Christian social ethic.

The formal aspects of social justice are considered to be secondary to the spiritual aspects of the Christian faith. The roots of this spiritualizing tendency among the German-speaking Mennonites in Lower South America can probably be traced, at least in part, to revivalistic influences from Europe and North America, as well as long contact with mainstream Protestantism in Europe (especially in the case of Uruguayan Mennonites of Prussian origin). For their part, the Spanish-speaking Mennonites

have been quite decisively influenced by the conserva-
tive-evangelical approach to the Christian life tradi-
tionally represented by denominations such as the Christian and Missionary Alliance, for example.

The spiritualistic vision of the Christian faith can also
be combined with a "Constantinian" vision of social
values. In Lower South America this orientation prevails
principally among Mennonites in South Brazil who are
currently benefiting from the expansionist economic
policies of that country, Paraguayan Mennonites whose
economic power is also growing, and Argentine Mennonites who are becoming quite well established in the
rising middle class.

(3) There is also an element of nonviolent social protest
committed to the struggle for social justice in the Mennonite Church in Lower South America represented ex-
plicitly by the Timbues Christian Community and,
perhaps implicity, by the Floresta congregation in
Montevideo and some Argentine congregations which
are experiencing charismatic renewal. However, there is
a difference between the orientation of these groups and
that which generally characterizes the International
Reconciliation Movements. It consists of the way in
which they begin with the church (congregation) as the
primary community in which God's justice is concretely
realized.

The Timbues Christian Community is located in a
socioeconomically marginal area in Montevideo. Its
people know firsthand the meaning of human misery
which results from the whole spectrum of socioeconomic
ills. Human frustration is vented in violent acts which are
in turn repressed with still greater violence. During
recent years members of the community have expressed

101

their social activism in a variety of ways which included leadership in community social service and action programs, creation of social consciousness, struggle for social justice through participation in the electoral process, participation in resistance groups of one type or another, etc. Gradually, perhaps through its experience of suffering, the community came to understand itself as a part of the people of God which is called to actually realize His justice. Their study of the Sermon on the Mount, lasting for nearly a year, culminated in an attempt to come to a consensus on a sociopolitical creed. Through this process some of the "members" were lost to the community. The life of the community is somewhat precarious, humanly speaking. Some have been arrested and even tortured for purposes of interrogation. One of the leaders of the congregation has been held without formal trial and sentencing for almost one year under suspicion of illegal association. Threats against the personal security of various members of the community are indications that the fundamentally nonviolent style of life and witness assumed by this community constitute an effective protest to social injustice. The spiritual resources available to the members of this worshiping and discipling brotherhood make it possible for them to absorb, in an extraordinary degree, the anger and violence directed against them in their struggle to be an expression of, and to bear witness to, God's will for human social relationships.

Toward a Strategy of Struggle for Social Justice Consistent with the Anabaptist Vision of the Church

It could be argued that the attempt to construct a strategy of struggle for social justice on the basis of the Anabaptist vision will prove to be a precarious undertaking. I recall having attended a meeting in Montevideo in which Jose Miguez Bonino reviewed critically an early book of Rubem Alves. Respondents were Julio de Santa Ana and Hugo Assmann. In his response, Santa Ana (who was then secretary of ISAL, a position now held by Assmann) made an impassioned plea that the "great representative Anabaptist, Thomas Muentzer" be taken more seriously by the church. It is apparent that one's own viewpoint tends to determine which of the Anabaptists he reads, as well as the way in which he interprets them. While I make no claim to full objectivity in the following paragraphs, I do feel that it is based on a generally accepted consensus of what the Anabaptists were about. The fact that an early ambivalence concerning the matter of violence gave way, in the crucible of this sixteenth-century struggle for social justice, to the renunciation of violent means, only strengthens the conviction that nonresistant suffering is fundamental to understanding the Anabaptist vision of the social justice issue.

(1) It implies, first of all, being a messianic community. An understanding of the church as a messianic community which is in fact the bearer of the real meaning of history, a paradigm of God's intention for all mankind, as well as the entire created order, is fundamental. The realization that it is by God's act of grace alone that this is so, will serve to keep the community humble. The fact that this reconciled and reconciling community is God's pattern for bringing to complete fulfillment His creation is the fundamental meaning and motivation for mission. Perhaps the most important task which confronts the church is simply resisting the seductive charms of the world, of being the church in spite of all of the pressures to force it into another mold. The fact that

103

it is already the community in which God's justice is being concretely realized gives it the moral right to denounce the deeds of tyrants, calling them to repentance in relation to specific injustices. Only a community which has been liberated by Christ can denounce with authority the idolatrous bondage to sacral systems. Only a community of reconciliation can denounce with authority the strife of nationalism, racism, and classism. Only the community of openness and honesty can denounce with any degree of credibility the deceitful and vicious uses of propaganda from both right and left. Only the community in which recourse to coercion has been renounced in an authentic brotherhood can with authority denounce the violence with which men persist in their evil desire to dominate their fellows.

(2) It implies being a community of testimony. The messianic community understands itself as the bearer of a liberating message. It is a matter of communicating a radically new way in human social relationships, rather than simply attempting to solve society's problems on the world's terms. Going beyond mere institutions of social service (worthy as these may be), going beyond mere programs of social action (strategic as these may be), the messianic community with its witness to a radically new way in human relationships serves society by raising consciousness in relation to social injustices and by contributing to the creation of social conscience. (This would seem to be the justification underlying the various forms of protest-witness such as symbolic actions, and the like.)

(3) The social strategy of the messianic community is determined concretely by the form which Jesus' messianic strategy took. According to the theocratic option,

the church acts in the world to change society. Christians see themselves as God's agents for ending injustices and bringing about social justice in the world. According to this vision a Christian minority, if it has access to power, can change society for the better. However, the messianic community is limited in the instruments which are at its disposal (those which the Messiah used) for bringing social change. Violence, defamation, falsehood, deceit, disrespect for persons, etc., are among the instruments which society has found to be most effective in expediting change. These are the instruments which have often been used (albeit grudgingly) by theocrats, as well. But they are not at the disposition of the messianic community because they do not partake of the essence of the messianic kingdom.

Negatively, the fact that the social strategy of the messianic community is determined by the form of messiahship which Jesus took upon Himself implies that coercive means which do violence to a person are not at the disposal of the church. Positively, it means that the "form of the servant" is the form which the messianic community takes. This fact, of course, determines the "what" of social concern as well as the "how" of social strategy of the messianic community in the world.

(4) The form of social concern in the messianic community is "servanthood." In our identification with Christ and His mission we become "servants." However, we should not confuse this "servanthood" with "service." "Service" tends to mean that which one does in the interests of the noble and just cause for which he is struggling. In reality, this may represent a theocratic orientation even though means may be nonviolent. "Servanthood" is symbolized in the church by the basin

105

and the towel and really amounts to a *form of being more than a strategy for doing*. "Servanthood" is the form which the community's concern for persons takes. Therefore the church will struggle to serve where social injustices are greatest and where human need is most acute. The lure to struggle at those points where the greatest strategic influence can be exercised is, in reality, a theocratic temptation. The messianic community is moved to struggle for social justice, not so much because of the amount of "good" that she can accomplish, but predominantly because she *is* a "servant" community. Being a "servant community" is the concrete way by which conformity to the messianic posture of Jesus in the world is realized by the church.

(5) The church is a sign, or a paradigm, of the kingdom in which concern for social justice is of necessity central. Therefore the struggle for justice moves us intensely, even though we resist the theocratic temptation to construct the kingdom in the world now by what appear to be the most efficacious means. (Perhaps we can say that watershed between the theocratic option and that of the messianic community in struggle for social justice lies at the point of willingness, or unwillingness, to sacrifice persons in the interests of a just cause.) We live and serve, we suffer and struggle in the confidence that God's kingdom will come. Meanwhile the messianic community furnishes models of God's justice in its radically new relationships, its servanthood service, its patient suffering which is the price of its costly discipleship. The church does not merely carry out these activities in order to pass the time until the kingdom comes. But rather, it is because the church is convinced that the form of the coming kingdom is already determined by the form of its

historic coming in the person of the Messiah. Therefore the coming of the kingdom will not be realized by means of coercion or violence, but in the actualization of the social relationships which correspond to the kingdom. A community which practices on a small scale the kind of social justice which is an essential part of the kingdom contributes a paradigmatic value to secular society. The role of the church is to be a foreign body within the larger body politic, whose mission is to show what the intention of God is for all mankind. Far from social ir-responsibility, this is the only way in which the com-munity of the Suffering Servant can be responsible.

Conclusion

In conclusion we offer several comments on the role of the missionary in the struggle for social justice in Latin America. No pretense is made to treat the subject in any depth, but rather to suggest several considerations which may merit further reflection.

(1) The missionary should be able to identify with understanding and sympathy with the national church to which he is sent in its struggle for social justice. In spite of the crusading fervor to which his prophetic vision may inspire him, on the one hand, and in spite of any personal nationalistic instincts which may conspire to make him defensive, on the other hand, the missionary should re-member that he is also part of a Latin American brotherhood whose vocation it is to discern the will of God in order to live in obedience. The missionary's primary contribution will be made in the context of the church. This role will be complicated by the widespread polarization over questions of social justice which already exist in the church. However, his humble contribution to

the process of discerning the disciple way of obedience will be important.

(2) The missionary also bears a responsibility toward the sending church in the developed world. The way in which Bartolome de las Casas literally shuttled back and forth between the new world and the old, between the colonies and the center of the empire, in order to lay the plight of the American peoples before the citizens of Spain and to plead in their behalf for social justice before the Council of the Indies, which administered the interests of Spain in the New World, speaks to the role of missionaries in this era of new imperial-colonial structures. Las Casas' message to the Indians was the liberating gospel of Jesus. His message to the rulers of Spain was the warning of coming judgment upon the nation for the injustices committed against the peoples of the New World.

Both parts of Las Casas' ministry were, in a fundamental sense, evangelization. To exploited peoples he preached the good news of the kingdom. He warned the Spaniards that selfish and violent men do not inherit the kingdom. There are times when the only possible way to proclaim the gospel is to warn of impending judgment. One wonders if this might not be a role which missionaries to the Third World should fill in the country from which they have been sent.

(3) One of the pressing issues of our time is whether a rich and powerful church can really communicate the gospel to poor and oppressed peoples. I believe that being a missionary in Latin America will require an evangelical witness of poverty as an expression of solidarity with the poor, with those who suffer as the result of social injustices. Christian poverty is an expression of love. It is

108

an expression of solidarity *with the poor* and *against poverty*.

In Latin America this solidarity means considerably more than living in economic austerity (although that is surely an important part). It will mean identifying with the oppressed, rather than with the oppressor. It means also the possibility of running risks in terms of personal safety, of being willing to put one's life on the line. (This is not a matter of mere abstract theory. We have colleagues who have assumed this commitment.) To renounce the recourse to the coercive exercise of power means also to assume the witness of poverty. And to take upon oneself the condition of evangelical poverty implies abandoning the recourse to violence which accompanies wealth.

Notes

1. Walter Klaassen pointed this out in a lecture on "Social Currents and Early Anabaptism" given at Goshen College (1975).

2. Reported by Bartolome de las Casas in *Historia de la Indias*, Book 5, ch. 4, quoted by Lewis Hanke, *The Spanish Struggle for Justice in the Conquest of America* (Philadelphia: University of Pennsylvania Press, 1949), p. 17.

3. Gustavo Gutierrez, *A Theology of Liberation; History, Politics, and Salvation.* Translated and edited by Sister Caridad Inda and John Eagleson (Maryknoll, New York: Orbis Books, 1973), p. ix.

4. *Ibid.,* p. 194.

5. For a critique of the Theology of Liberation and an evaluation of its strengths and weaknesses see Orlando E. Costas, *The Church and Its Mission: A Shattering Critique from the Third World* (Wheaton, Ill.: Tyndale House Publishers, 1974), pp. 250 ff.

6. "Justice in the World," Doc. II.1, a statement prepared by the Catholic bishops of Peru. *IDOC-North America,* "The Future of the Missionary Enterprise," Number 51/March 1973, pp. 21-24.

7. *Ibid.*, p. 23.

8. Father Domingo Lain, "An Open Letter to the People of Colombia," Doc. II.8, *IDOC-North America, ibid.*, pp. 35-37.

9. Johann and Hildegard Goss-Mayer, "Efforts for Liberation by Non-Violence in Latin America," *IDOC-North America, ibid.*, p. 26.

10. Joseph S. McCullough, a letter published in *IDOC-North America, ibid.*, p. 28.

John Driver   Samuel Escobar

Samuel Escobar was born in Peru and attended a British missionary school in Arequipa. He received his MA degree in Arts and Education from the San Marcos University in Lima in 1956, following which he taught at elementary, secondary, and university levels.

In 1959 Escobar became a traveling secretary with the International Fellowship of Evangelical Students (IFES) which took him to practically every country in Latin America. Some years later he pursued doctoral studies in philosophy at the University of Madrid and eventually served as secretary of the Inter-Varsity Christian Fellowship (IVCF) based in Toronto.

Escobar is well-known in Western evangelical and ecumenical circles as lecturer at youth meetings, the Lausanne Congress on Evangelism, and other occasions. The Escobar chapters in this book were given at the Associated Mennonite Biblical Seminaries in Elkhart, Indiana, in connection with the annual Mennonite Missionary Fellowship sessions in 1975. He is also author of *Dialogo entre Cristo y Marx* (Lima, 1967, 1969) and *Decadencia de la Religion* (Buenos Aires, 1972), as well as of numerous chapters in books and journal articles. Escobar continues to serve as president of the Latin American

111

Theological Fraternity and as [1] director of the Kairos Theological Community in Buenos Aires.

The Escobars currently make their home in Cordoba, Argentina, with their two children, Lilly Ester and Alejandro. In a recent communication Samuel Escobar wrote: "I am in fellowship with the Plymouth Brethren now, but I describe myself as an Anabaptist."

John Driver grew up in Hesston, Kansas, where he graduated from Hesston Academy. He received his BA from Goshen College, Goshen, Indiana, in 1950, his BD from Goshen Biblical Seminary in 1960, and his STM from Perkins School of Theology, Dallas, Texas, in 1967. He married Bonita Landis. They are the parents of Cynthia, Wilfred, and Jonathan.

The Drivers have been working as part of the Mennonite Board of Missions (Elkhart, Indiana) Latin team since 1951. Earlier, John served with Mennonite Central Committee and Mennonite Relief Committee in Puerto Rico from 1945 to 1948 and Bonita from 1947 to 1948. They then served as missionaries in Puerto Rico from 1951 to 1966 and in Uruguay from 1967 to 1974.

As part of his missionary assignment in Uruguay, John Driver was professor of church history and New Testament at the Seminario Evangelico Menonita de Teologia, Montevideo. He also served the seminary until its closing in late 1974 as dean of studies from 1967, and as acting rector from 1972. Since 1975 the Drivers have spent most of their time establishing a Mennonite witness in Spain.

John Driver is the author of *Community and Commitment* (Herald Press, 1976), which had first appeared as *Comunidad y Compromiso* in Argentina in 1974, as well as numerous journal and periodical articles. His contribution to this book was first presented in the annual meeting of the Mennonite Missionary Fellowship at the Associated Mennonite Biblical Seminaries in 1975.